DOCUMENTS OF MODERN HISTORY

General Editors:

A. G. Dickens

The Director, Institute of Historical Research, University of London

Alun Davies

Professor of Modern History, University College, Swansea

GOVERNMENT AND SOCIETY IN FRANCE
1814–1848

edited by

Irene Collins
Senior Lecturer in History,
University of Liverpool

New York · St. Martin's Press

© Irene Collins, 1970

First Published 1970

First published in
the United States of America in 1971
by St. Martin's Press, Inc.,
175 Fifth Avenue, New York, New York

First published in Great Britain by
Edward Arnold (Publishers) Limited

Library of Congress Catalog Card Number: 78-143997

Printed in Great Britain by
Robert Cunningham and Sons Ltd., Alva

CONTENTS

ACKNOWLEDGMENTS

The editor and publishers wish to thank the following for their pemission to quote from copyright sources: Editions A. & J. Picard (**V, 5**); Librarie Générale de Droit et de Jurisprudence (**I, 1, 3**) (**III, 1, 5**); Presses Universitaires de France (**III, 6**), and Annales de la Faculte des Lettres (**VIII, 2**).

INTRODUCTION

Documentary sources inevitably reflect most clearly the interests and opinions of the literate. What proportion of the French nation could be thus described? The Charter of 1814 (**I, 3**) made no promise of universal education. Restoration governments, perhaps because industry was little developed or because they were already embarrassed by a superfluity of émigrés looking for jobs, did not seem to think it mattered that the majority of people could neither read nor write: in 1825 more than half the communes in France lacked any sort of school. The revised Charter of 1830 (**VII, 3**) expressed a true purpose of amendment, and the bourgeoisie of the July Monarchy laboured hard to fulfil the promise (**XI**). If their chief incentive was the selfish one of making the poor less dangerous and more industrious, at least they never doubted, as many Englishmen at the time doubted, that popular education was a public benefit. In Paris and some other large towns they ran successful courses for adults as well as schools for children, but in the countryside they made little headway against the peasant mentality (**XI, 3**). According to the unreliable statistics of the time the number of those who could read and write was just beginning to outstrip the number of the totally illiterate when Louis-Philippe's reign was approaching its end.

How many people, then, read the newspapers so frequently quoted in this book? During the Restoration, French newspapers, though cheaper than those in England, were considered dear, and they could only be bought on a quarterly subscription basis. Some daily newspapers had a mere 2,000 subscribers; the *Quotidienne* (**II, 3**) was considered reasonably successful with 5,000; the *Journal des Débats* (**I, 2; VI, 1**) excelled itself with 13,000; the *Constitutionnel* (**IV, 2**) was a source of fear and wonder with 20,000. Numbers did not increase spectacularly during the July Monarchy, even though Émile de Girardin showed with his *Presse* (**IX, 1a**) in 1836 that it was possible to halve the price and make up the deficit with advertisements. The *Presse* had only 13,000 subscribers in 1841, the *Constitutionnel* 24,000 in 1843. Circulation varied enormously from one part of the country to another. In 1830 there were five departments which received each 300 copies of the *Constitutionnel* alone, and seven others which took between them less than 200 copies of all nineteen national dailies put together.

Even so, newspapers were considered a power in the land. The press department of the Ministry of the Interior bristled with figures and reports on them; Villèle regarded them as responsible for blackening his scheme to indemnify the émigrés; Guizot spent large sums of money in attempts to found a ministerial organ. All governments, even those which adopted a liberal attitude towards the press in general, were determined to control newspapers by one means or another (**I, 5; III, 2; VIII, 4**). This was partly because people remembered with horror the demagogic newspapers of the Revolution; partly because the novelty of regular elections made politicians unusually conscious of opinion; and partly because newspaper employees formed, along with students, the biggest collections of informed citizens. It was journalists who provoked the assault on Charles X in 1830 (**VI, 4b**), typographers and the like who began building the barricades, and journalists again who whipped up the demonstration leading to the fall of the July Monarchy (**XIV, 5a**).

Of the literate, how many were interested in the parliamentary proceedings on which historians place so much importance? In 1814, British and other allied leaders were exasperated with the French because they did not seem to care what sort of government they got. Louis XVIII believed he must rule with a parliament, so the text of the Charter was 'flung together', in Beugnot's famous words, 'like the libretto of a comic opera'. Few people noticed that Louis had evaded the attempt to make him a popular nominee (**I, 1, 3**) and that the preamble and signature described him as king by Divine Right over the past nineteen years (**I, 3**). Articles 38 to 40, elaborated by a franchise law in 1817, gave political rights to very few people: by 1830, out of a population of 29 million, only 16,000 were eligible for parliament and 90,000 for the vote. Moreover, they were all very wealthy, except for the few brought in by virtue of article 39 from poor departments such as Corsica; and a large proportion of them, due to the incidence of direct taxes, were great landowners.

In spite of all this, newspapers saw fit to devote the greater part of their columns to political discussion; and according to police reports, newspapers were avidly consulted in libraries and reading rooms by people too poor to buy them. In 1819 a rumour that the government was about to tamper with the electoral system brought petitions pouring into the Chamber, from artisans and peasants who had no ambitions to vote themselves. This was because the maintenance of parliamentary government as established in 1814 had come to be regarded as essential to the maintenance of other rights also promised in

1814 and more widely cherished: equal justice, equal taxes, equal opportunity of employment, the inviolability of property – in short, the promise that aristocracy and clergy would never return to the privileged position they had enjoyed before the Revolution. Should they do so, men might lose both their land and their jobs. Hence the intense fears aroused by Villèle's penchant for the old nobility (**III, 4**), the acute sensitivity concerning the fortunes of national land (**I, 4; III, 7**), and the absorbing attention paid to the relationship between church and state (**IV**). The aristocracy would seem in some ways to have been the greater threat, since they never constituted less than 40 per cent of the membership of any Chamber of the Restoration; but the clergy were more ubiquitous in the countryside, and anti-clericalism in consequence became the dominant theme of the times.

Louis XVIII, up to the last few months of his reign, was an old-fashioned sceptic who could be relied upon to keep priests at arms' length, but Charles X was a different cup of tea (**III, 6**). Hence, the power which in Louis's hands had seemed a desirable check upon demagogues looked suddenly menacing. Charles was lavish in assurances that he would respect the Charter, and in fact he never openly contravened it as Louis and his last parliament did with the Septennial Act (**III, 5**), but there were many ways in which he might pervert the spirit whilst obeying the letter. Chateaubriand pointed out in 1814 that the Charter could practically be destroyed by virtue of its own fourteenth article, which gave the king the right to rule by decree. The situation with regard to ministers was ambiguous: according to article 13 they were 'responsible', but to whom and in what sense? The Charter itself spoke only of legal sanctions (articles 55 and 56). In 1816, Liberals protected Louis's right to choose his own ministers (**II, 1**) because in their opinion he chose better men than would have emerged from the parliamentary (ultra-royalist) majority: in 1830 the self-same Liberals subscribed to an address (**VI, 3b**) which could only have been an appeal to the King to accept the dictates of parliament (though their lawyer Dupin afterwards denied that it was any such thing), because Charles's choice was far outside the circle of acceptable politicians (**VI, 1**). The deadlock in 1830 between the king's ministers and the elected Chamber, which Royer-Collard had thought could never arise (**II, 1**), brought up the whole question of sovereign authority so lightly passed over in 1814. Had the king granted the Charter from a plenitude of power, or had it been offered to him by the sovereign nation? Newspapers and pamphlets debated the issue day after day and week after week, repeating the same arguments, the same recriminations, the same gloomy prognostications in a manner which would have astonished later generations. In the end the *coup d'état* (**VI, 4**) was a surprise to no-one.

With the advent of Louis-Philippe the political élite was widened somewhat. Articles 38 to 40 of the revised Charter, elaborated by the franchise law of 1831, made 174,000 people eligible for the vote (increasing to 248,000 by 1848) and 15,000 eligible for parliament. The vast majority still qualified by means of the taxes which they paid on land, but it should not be assumed that they were all farmers or idle rich. In the Chamber of 1840, 137 out of 459 deputies had no other occupation than landowning, but another 175 were civil servants, 87 were lawyers, teachers, writers or doctors, and 60 were bankers, manufacturers or merchants. By now, however, the proceedings of parliament were said to be boring and without relevance to the important issues of the day (**IX, 1**). With the defeat of the ultra-royalist party the old divisive issues had gone, and nobody outside parliament cared much whether Soult was in and Molé out or vice versa, since all the new politicians looked much alike. The activities of political minorities could arouse passions on both sides (**VIII**), but on the whole politics had lost their interest. This was probably the reason why the majority of newspapers, remaining obstinately political, failed to expand their readership in those days of apparently widening opportunity. Even the *National*, which played so large a part in both revolutions (**VI, 4b; XIV, 5a**), had less than 5,000 subscribers in the 1840s.

A few newspapers achieved more spectacular figures by publishing serial stories, the most popular being those which exploited the new interest in the poor (**XIII, 4**). By the 1840s this was undoubtedly the predominant theme in literature of all kinds. The voluminous social surveys of the period (**XII**) give the historian some insight into the conditions prevailing among the poor, but in spite of the fact that most of the writers were inspired by an earnest wish to do good, their attitude was still that of the more fortunate. French writers on social problems, like most English, believed that the difficulties under which the poor laboured were aggravated and partly caused by their own fecklessness and vice; and they had less faith than the English, perhaps because of their comparative lack of evangelical zeal, in the capacity of the poor for redemption. They were obsessed by conditions in towns, and by the appearance of a new phenomenon, for which there was a new word, pauperism. Poverty due to food shortage or land hunger was well known, and the Bible said that the poor were always with us; but a state of destitution affecting whole classes of the population and apparently necessary to the prosperity of other classes, was new, and a consequence of the development of mechanised industry. Most people who heard of it were very shocked, though few could think of a remedy. Some, like Saint-Marc Girardin (**XIII,3a**), regarded it as the greatest threat to the established order, forgetting that the silk weavers of Lyon who rebelled in 1831 belonged to an older type of poor, like the Parisian sans-culottes. It was the latter who ultimately proved to be the more dangerous. It was they, headed by the little craftsmen such as read the *Atelier* (**XIII, 2a**), who most bitterly resented the new class distinctions based on the belief that the poor were a different kind of human being from the rich (**XIII, 3b**). They were not the poorest of the poor: it was out of resentment as much as poverty that they rebelled in 1848.

Meanwhile the very poor, in both town and country, remained as inarticulate as ever, and the historian scarcely hears a word from them except when they got into the law courts. The pages of the *Gazette des Tribuneaux* form an excellent source of social history, not least because of the facetious terms in which the writers saw fit to report quite pathetic cases (**XIII, 2b**).

Politics recovered their interest for many people when the hue and cry broke out against corruption in 1847. Attacks on electoral chicanery had long been the stock-in-trade of opposition deputies and journalists, but they had failed to arouse much interest outside the narrow ranks of defeated candidates and defrauded electors (**IX, 2b**). The bargaining which went on at elections was a subject of derision (**IX, 3**), but there is no evidence that peasants and townsmen did anything but take advantage of the pig-markets, civic centres and town-hall clocks which their electors won for them. Corruption on a grand scale in very high places was another matter. It affected the national honour, and Frenchmen, especially in towns (witness the *Atelier* in 1840, **X, 5**), were very sensitive about the nation's honour. Like most forms of nationalism it gave a feeling of status to a great mass of lower middle-class citizens who had neither careers, possessions nor political powers to glory in. It was the revelation of great scandals (**XIV, 2**) which gave a fillip to the banquet campaign of 1847 (**XIV, 1**) and which made Louis-Philippe's natural supporters among the bourgeoisie too sheepish to defend him.

France during the period covered by this book was a much administered country. During the early years of the Restoration, Liberals attacked officialdom and asked for more elected bodies (**II, 2; II, 4**), but when it came to the point they balked at losing the greatest legacy of Napoleonic rule, bureaucratic efficiency. Mayors and their deputies continued to be appointed and paid, postal services were increased, the state education system was extended; by 1839 France had 130,000 civil servants. Communications between officials (**V, 1; V, 3; V, 4; VIII, 2; IX, 2a; XIV, 2**) were as typical of life under the constitutional monarchy as parliamentary speeches, and it is not inappropriate that the quarrel which sparked off the revolution of 1848 should have concerned the right of the police to interfere with a public meeting (**XIV, 5**).

In many accounts the history of this period is divided into two parts, as though there had been a dramatic change in 1830. Casimir Périer would have resisted any such interpretation (**VIII, 1**); the Revolution of 1830, he said, had changed nothing but the dynasty. Radicals would have resisted it too, for as far as they could see the vast mass of Frenchmen were no nearer to power or prosperity (**VII, 4**). There were many ways in which life went on as usual. The electoral pressure exerted by ministers under the July Monarchy (**IX, 2a**) was no greater than that employed by Decazes and Villèle, and the social conditions revealed under Louis-Philippe had been witnessed by Villeneuve-Bargemont under Charles X (**XII, 1**). Yet with the departure of the old nobility, the atmosphere of public life was different – less romantic and traditional, more materialistic and immediate. The spectacular amateurs like Chateaubriand (**III, 3**), whose unsuitable temperament did so much to ruin Villèle's efforts to make the ultra-royalists into a sound governing party, gave way to a race of professional politicians like Duchâtel and Guizot, who sacrificed policy to the interests of maintaining a working majority. The formal speeches of the Restoration, composed beforehand with an eye to publication, were not often emulated in the Chambers of the July Monarchy: the memorable speeches were now spontaneous and impressionistic, like Lamartine's and De Tocqueville's (**IX, 1b; XIV, 4**). Whereas Royer-Collard's philosophizing won universal respect in the Chambre Introuvable, Guizot's heavy generalizations provoked a good deal of irritation a generation later. Though all styles have lost a good deal in translation, they may still serve to illustrate the richness of oratory which was one of the outstanding features of political life in France under her last three kings.

I

BOURBON MONARCHY TWICE RESTORED

1 The Senate's proposal for a constitution, 6 April 1814

On 31 March 1814 allied armies marched into Paris. Beyond a determination to secure the abdication of Napoleon, the leaders were undecided about France's future government. On 2 April Talleyrand, Napoleon's former foreign secretary, assembled such of Napoleon's senators as remained in Paris and persuaded them that if they took the initiative in restoring a Bourbon king they might secure guarantees for themselves. They drew up a constitution which provided for parliamentary government and personal liberties, and included the following significant clauses.

Article 1. The French government is monarchic, and succession shall be by order of primogeniture in the male line.

Article 2. The French people freely summon to the throne of France Louis-Stanislas-Xavier de France, brother of the late king, and after him the other members of the House of Bourbon in the old order. . . .

Article 6. There shall be at least one hundred and fifty senators, and at most two hundred. . . . Existing senators, with the exception of those who shall have renounced their status as French citizens, shall be retained and included in this number. . . .

Article 29. The present consitution shall be submitted for the acceptance of the French people in the form to be prescribed. Louis-Stanislas-Xavier shall be proclaimed *King of the French* on taking oath and signing a declaration in the following terms: 'I hereby accept the constitution, and I swear that I will observe it and see that it is observed by others.' This oath shall be repeated at the solemn ceremony at which he receives the oath of allegiance of the French people.

L. Duguit and H. Monnier, *Les Constitutions et les principales lois politiques de la France depuis 1789* (6th ed., Paris, 1943) pp. 359-62

2 The new king

With the fall of Napoleon, the *Journal de l'Empire*, which had been a royalist newspaper at the time of the Revolution, took back its royalist editors, the brothers Bertin, and changed its title to *Journal des Débats*. Efforts were made to collect information about the new king, who had left France as long ago as 1789, and to present him in a favourable light to middle class readers brought up to distrust him.

His Majesty King Louis XVIII lived for some time in the manor house of Hartwell, in Buckinghamshire, about 40 miles from London.[1] His Majesty has always enjoyed good health. In appearance he has changed little, being still handsome and prepossessing[2]: one sees in him that air of kindliness which characterized his august brother, Louis XVI. His Majesty often took the pleasure of walking out, and often of riding. Whenever he approached a town or passed through a village, all the bells would ring out to welcome him, and the inhabitants would rush out to meet him, following him and overwhelming him with expressions of love and veneration. Hartwell and its beautiful grounds were given to His Majesty by the owner. From the first His Majesty treated the inhabitants with the greatest kindness. He lightened all their burdens, and even sought out the poor in their humble homes, drying the tears of the unfortunate. Amongst them His Majesty was like a father with his children.

His Majesty had the good fortune in this land of exile, which was withal a land of hospitality, to have with him several members of his august family: the Comte d'Artois,[3] the Duc d'Angoulême,[4] the Duc de Berry,[5] and the Duchesse d'Angoulême.[6] The Duchess, especially,

---

[1] Hartwell House, near Aylesbury, the property of the Rev. Sir George Lee, was oaned to Louis XVIII in 1810 and remained the seat of the French royal family until 1814.

[2] Louis at the Restoration was 58 years old, enormously fat, and incapable of rising from a chair without assistance.

[3] Louis's brother, later Charles X (b. 1757; d. 1836).

[4] Eldest son of the Comte d'Artois (1775-1844).

[5] Second son of the Comte d'Artois (1778-1820).

[6] Daughter of Louis XVI and Marie Antoinette (1778-1851).

lavished all the attentions of a loving daughter on the King. These illustrious refugees, these noble sons of France, showed affectionate concern for the lot of French prisoners, and distributed aid amongst them; the Duchess, particularly, gave them all she possessed. In this way, through the medium of good deeds, she was able to draw near, at least in thought, to the homeland which she always missed, and which she still loved with all her heart. Later, His Majesty lost the company of the princes, who went to prepare the way for his return to the throne of his ancestors.[7] The king himself left his abode and proceeded to London, and it is from there that in a few days' time His Majesty will depart, amid the acclamations of a hospitable people, whose feelings of regret will follow him, to return to the soil of France, where a people too long repressed will hail him, with ecstacies of joy, King of France and father of their country.[8]

But let us return to the simple occupations of His Majesty during his retirement. He improved the time by the study of literature, which had always been his favourite pastime even in his most prosperous days. Much could be said about the extent and variety of his knowledge, about his retentive memory, and about the perceptiveness which enabled him to grasp swiftly but surely the significance and purport of a subject. Mention could be made of His Majesty's love of the arts, of the special study he has made of them, and of the facility, eloquence and precision with which he can speak about them. But these are the qualities of the man: we would speak now of the virtues of the monarch.

Enveloped, if we may put it that way, in the spying and the snares of Bonapartist agents, our king had to gather up and concentrate into his own hands all the business that required attention. In fact it was he alone who opened and read despatches and he alone who wrote replies. If there were envoys of foreign powers and their governments to be received, it was the king who interviewed them, took the reports they had brought with them, and gave his replies either verbally or in writing. A king who has been endowed with such an extensive training as His Majesty, and who, in his wisdom and prudence, has condescended to study all aspects of political science down to the minutest detail, must today have the most profound knowledge, both of men and affairs, that anyone could possibly acquire.

Such is the Sovereign whom the King of Kings has nurtured amid the

---

[7] Angoulême entered Bordeaux, after it had been taken by Wellington, on 12 March 1814. Artois, who had joined the Austrian army in eastern France, entered Paris on 12 April and was proclaimed provisional head of the government by the Senate.
[8] He left Hartwell on 19 April only, and embarked on 24 April.

tempests of Europe, and amid the tribulations sent him in God's mercy to make him a perfect prince: a sovereign who combines goodness with strength and is capable both of ensuring the prosperity and happiness of France during many years of peace and of defending her, by strong but wise government, from past mistakes and future errors.

Long live Louis XVIII !

Journal des Débats, 18 April 1814

3   The Charter, 4 June 1814

Louis was unwilling to impair his sovereign authority by accepting a constitution from the hands of the Senate. On his arrival in Paris he worked out a draft of his own, and submitted it to a committee consisting of nine members of the Senate, nine members of the Legislative Body, and three royal commissioners (Montesquiou, Beugnot, and Ferrand). The committee made few alterations. On 4 June the constitution or 'Charter' was read out to the Senate and the Legislative Body, which became the Chamber of Peers and the Chamber of Deputies of the new régime. The preamble, which had not been discussed by the committee, was presumably added by the king.

Divine Providence, in bringing us back to our realm after a long absence, has imposed great obligations upon us. Peace was the primary need of our subjects, and this we have worked at without respite. The peace that was so essential for France and for the whole of Europe has now been signed.[9] The present state of our kingdom made a constitutional charter desirable: this we have promised, and this we now publish. We have borne in mind that, although complete authority in France is vested in the person of the king, our predecessors did not hesitate to modify the exercise of that authority in accordance with prevailing conditions. Thus the communes owed their independence to Louis the Fat and the confirmation and extension of their rights to Saint Louis and Philip the Fair; the judicial order was established and developed by laws of Louis XI, Henry II and Charles IX; and finally Louis XIV regulated almost all aspects of public administration in a series of ordinances whose wisdom has never been surpassed. Like our predecessors we have had to weigh the effects of the constant progress of knowledge. . . . We have recognized that in desiring a constitutional charter our subjects were expressing a real need; but in granting their desire we have taken every precaution to ensure that the charter was

---

[9] Treaties between France and the four Great Powers were signed on 30 May. Treaties with Sweden, Portugal and Spain were signed on 8 and 12 June and 20 July.

worthy of us and of the people we are proud to command . . . . While realizing that a free and monarchical constitution would fulfil the expectations of enlightened Europe, we have also had to remember that our first duty to our people was to maintain, in their own interests, the rights and prerogatives of the crown. We hoped that experience may have convinced them that only the supreme authority can give to the institutions which it has established the force, permanence, and majesty with which it is itself invested; and that when, therefore, the wisdom of kings is in agreement with the wishes of the people a constitutional charter may be long lasting, but when concessions are extracted by violence from a weak government the liberty of the people is just as much in danger as the throne itself. Finally we have looked for the principles of our constitutional charter in the character of the French people and in the venerable relics of past centuries. For instance, we have regarded the renewal of the peerage as a truly national institution, and one that should link up past memories with present hopes, re-uniting the old with the new. We have put a Chamber of Deputies in place of those ancient assemblies of Champ de Mars and Champ de Mai and those assemblies of the Third Estate, which so often gave proof at one and the same time of their zeal in the cause of the people and of their fidelity and respect towards the authority of the king. In seeking thus to re-forge the links of time, which fatal departures have broken, we have effaced from our memory all the evils which have afflicted our country during our absence, as we would wish that they could be erased from the pages of history.

For these reasons we have voluntarily, and through the free exercise of our royal authority, granted and do hereby grant, concede and bestow upon our subjects, on behalf of ourself and our successors for ever, the following constitutional charter:

Public Law of the French

1. Frenchmen are equal before the law, whatever may be their rank and title.
2. They shall contribute without discrimination, in proportion to their income, towards the expenses of the state.
3. They shall all be equally admissible to civil and military posts.
4. Their personal liberty is likewise guaranteed; no-one shall be prosecuted or arrested except in cases provided for by law and in the form which it prescribes.
5. All men may profess their religion with equal freedom, and shall obtain for their worship the same protection.

6. The Roman Catholic and Apostolic religion shall, however, be the state religion.

7. Ministers of the Roman Catholic and Apostolic religion, and those of other Christian denominations, shall receive stipends from the state.

8. Frenchmen have the right to publish and print their opinions, as long as they conform to the laws for repressing abuses of this liberty.

9. All property is inviolable, including that which is called *national*,[10] the law making no distinction between them.

10. The state can require the sacrifice of property on account of a legally established public interest, but only with a previous indemnity.

11. Investigation into opinions and votes given prior to the Restoration is forbidden. . . .

12. Conscription is abolished. The method of recruiting for the army and navy shall be determined by law.[11]

Forms of the king's government

13. The person of the king is inviolable and sacred. His ministers shall be responsible. To the king alone belongs the executive power.

14. The king is the supreme head of the state. He shall command the land and sea forces, declare war, make treaties of peace, alliance and commerce, appoint to all positions in the public administration, and make such rules and ordinances as are necessary for the execution of the laws and the safety of the state.

15. The legislative power shall be exercised collectively by the king, the Chamber of Peers, and the Chamber of Deputies.

16. The king shall initiate legislation.

17. Bills shall be presented first either to the Chamber of Peers or to the Chamber of Deputies, as the king wishes; with the exception of finance bills, which must be presented first to the Chamber of Deputies.

18. Every law must be freely debated, and passed by the majority of each of the two Chambers.

19. The Chambers shall have power to petition the king to present a bill on any subject, and to indicate what provisions they think the bill should contain. . . .

22 The king alone can sanction and promulgate laws.

23. The civil list shall be fixed for the whole of the reign, by the first legislature to meet after the accession of the king.

---

[10] Property confiscated from church and émigrés during the Revolution and sold by the state to private owners.

[11] The required law was produced on 10 March 1818. It virtually re-established conscription, but allowed more exemptions than Napoleon had allowed during the last years of the Empire.

The Chamber of Peers

27. The king has the right to appoint peers. The number he can appoint is unlimited. . . .

28. Peers shall be entitled to enter the Chamber at 25 years of age and to speak and vote at 30.

32. All sittings of the Chamber of Peers shall be held *in camera*.

33. The Chamber of Peers shall possess jurisdiction over crimes of high treason and attacks upon the security of the state, as defined by law. . . .

The Chamber of Deputies

35. The Chamber of Deputies shall be composed of deputies chosen by electoral colleges, whose organisation shall be determined by law.

36. Each department shall have the number of deputies it has had up to now.[12]

37. Deputies shall be elected for five years, in such a manner that the Chamber is renewed by one fifth each year.

38. No deputy shall be admitted to the Chamber unless he is 40 years of age and pays 1,000 francs in direct taxes.

39. If, however, a department cannot provide 50 persons of the required age who pay at least 1,000 francs in direct taxes, the number shall be made up from the largest taxpayers below the 1,000 franc level.

40. Electors of deputies must pay direct taxes to the sum of 300 francs and be at least 30 years of age.

41. Presidents of electoral colleges shall be appointed by the king, and shall be *ex officio* members of the college.

42. At least half of the deputies shall be chosen from eligible candidates who have their political domicile in the department.[13]

43. The president of the Chamber of Deputies shall be appointed by the king, from a list of 5 members presented by the Chamber.

46. No amendment can be made to a bill unless it has been proposed or accepted by the king. . . .

48. No tax can be imposed or collected unless it has been agreed to by the Chambers and sanctioned by the king.

49. The land tax shall be voted for one year only. Indirect taxes can be voted for several years.

50. The king shall convoke the two Chambers annually; he can pro-

---

[12] By the constitution of 1802, seats were allocated to the departments in accordance with their population. The number of deputies for the area which France retained at the Restoration was 257.

[13] i.e. pay some of their taxes by virtue of property situated there.

rogue them and dissolve that of the Deputies, but in such a case he must convoke a new one within the space of three months. . . .

52. No member of the Chamber can be prosecuted or arrested on a criminal charge during the course of a session without the Chamber's permission, unless he be taken in the act.

53. No petition can be brought or presented to either Chamber except in writing. . . .

Ministers

54. Ministers can be members of either the Chamber of Peers or the Chamber of Deputies. They can, in addition, enter either Chamber, and they must be given a hearing when they demand it.

55. The Chamber of Deputies has the right to accuse ministers and to arraign them before the Chamber of Peers, which alone has the right of trying them.

56. They cannot be accused except in the event of treason or peculation. Special laws shall define the nature of these offences and determine the form of prosecution.

The Judiciary

57. All justice emanates from the king. It shall be administered in his name by judges nominated and authorized by him.

58. Judges appointed by the king are irremovable.

59. The courts and regular tribunals at present in existence shall be maintained. There shall be no change except by virtue of a law.

60. The existing commercial jurisdiction shall be maintained.

61. The commission of the peace shall be retained. Justices of the peace, although appointed by the king, are not irremovable.

62. No-one can be deprived of his natural judges.

63. In consequence, extraordinary commissions and tribunals cannot be created. Provost courts are not included in this category if their re-establishment should be judged necessary.[14]

64. Criminal trials shall be public unless such publicity would be dangerous to order and morality, in which case the tribunal concerned shall declare it to be so by judicial order.

65. The jury system shall be retained. . . .

66. The penalty of confiscation of property is abolished and cannot be re-established.

67. The king has the right to pardon, and to commute penalties.

---

[14] These were semi-military courts used for the trial of civilians. They were set up temporarily by a law of 20 December 1815.

Special rights guaranteed by the state

69. Persons on active military service, retired officers and soldiers, and pensioned widows shall retain their ranks, honours and pensions.

70. The national debt is guaranteed.

71. Members of the old nobility shall resume their titles, and of the new retain theirs. The king shall make nobles at will, but he shall grant them only rank and honours, without any exemption from the burdens and duties of society.

72. The Legion of Honour shall be maintained. . . .

73. The colonies shall be governed by special laws and regulations.

74. The king and his successors shall swear, in the solemn service of their consecration, to observe this constitutional charter faithfully.

Given at Paris, in the year of our Lord one thousand eight hundred and fourteen, and of our reign the nineteenth.

Signed: Louis

L. Duguit and H. Monnier, *op. cit.*, pp. 363-9

4   The Second Restoration, July 1815

Government was barely organized when Napoleon escaped from Elba and Louis XVIII fled the country. On being restored to the throne a second time, after France's defeat at Waterloo, the king allowed his friends and supporters to carry out reprisals. Officials who had served Napoleon too conspicuously fled or were dismissed: between 50,000 and 80,000 people lost their jobs. The merest signs of Bonapartist allegiance were proscribed. White terrorists were allowed and even encouraged to carry out vengeance, not only for the Hundred Days but for the Revolution: untold numbers of people were murdered, especially in southern France. The following extracts from a local newspaper give some idea of how the change of régime was effected in one comparatively peaceful area. The *Journal de la Côte d'Or*, like most provincial newspapers at this time, could only survive financially by publishing official communications and thereby earning a little money from government funds.

From the prefect of the department of the Côte d'Or to all those under his administration

Citizens,

The days of trouble and anxiety are at last coming to an end. The king is in his capital in the heart of France. He has again removed the scourge of war from our country. At peace with the whole of Europe, he is again reconciling us with all nations, putting a stop to bloodshed and bringing to an end an invasion too terrifying to think of – an invasion by forces never before equalled in the history of mankind.

True to his promises this good king assures us once more of all the advantages of the constitutional charter. Civil liberty is more secure than ever. Citizens are equal in the eyes of the law and will never have anything to fear from a government whose sole purpose is to protect them from the tyranny which, disguised under many different names, has oppressed us for the last twenty-four years. Property is assured, *national land is guaranteed*, confiscation has been abolished. Frenchmen may, if they wish, be the happiest people on earth.

Let us then enjoy, at last, this new order of things. Let us await patiently the alleviations and improvements which it will certainly bring but which cannot be realized in a day. Let us turn a deaf ear to false insinuations regarding the re-establishment of tithes and feudal rights, the absurdity of which is manifest. Citizens of the Côte d'Or, put your full trust in the best of kings, relying on his care and consideration. Be calm in the circumstances which have arisen, and respect persons and property. Abstain from all words and actions that might prejudice public order and your own peace and safety, and have confidence in your magistrates, whose duty and desire is always to protect your interests. Long live the king!

Dijon, 11 July 1815

Signed: Petitot, Councillor acting on behalf of the prefect[15]

The prefect of the department of the Côte d'Or,

Considering that it is the duty of magistrates to suppress all symbols of allegiance that are not in accordance with the general will and that are used by agitators to mislead people and disturb the peace;

Considering that His Majesty does not regard as representative of the nation the wish expressed by some citizens to keep the tricolour cockade, when in every department the vast majority of citizens have spontaneously adopted the white cockade, the symbol of peace, order, tranquillity, and loyal support for the government, HEREBY DECREES

1. Any tricolour flags that may still be found, either at the top of church towers or in front of town halls or other public buildings, shall at once be removed and replaced by white flags.

2. Mayors, police superintendents, and their deputies in rural communes are called upon and if necessary ordered to arrest and prosecute, with all

---

[15] A new prefect, Bercagny, had been appointed by Napoleon during the Hundred Days. He fled the department when Louis XVIII re-entered Paris.

the vigour of the law, any person found wearing any symbol other than the white cockade.

3. They are also called upon to prosecute in like manner any person who attempts to disturb the peace under the pretext of forcing others to wear the white cockade.

Dijon, 11 July 1815

Signed: Petitot, Councillor acting on behalf of the prefect

News of the Department, 19 July 1815:

Under a decree issued yesterday by the prefect of the Côte d'Or, M. Coste, mayor of Saint-Jean-de-Lône, was suspended from office. He has been replaced provisionally by M. Adeline, solicitor and notary, who will bring to the administration quite a different spirit from that of his predecessor. . . . At Auxonne M. Demoisy, solicitor and notary, is acting as mayor for the time being. M. Malot, apothecary, is deputy mayor and M. Briseville, officer of dragoon guards (retired) has replaced the police superintendent in a temporary capacity. These appointments will help considerably to reform persons led astray by the late administration. . . .

The survivors of the partisan corps spewed up by the Department of the Côte d'Or are still carrying on the brigandage that the corps went in for during the fighting. They are stealing considerable sums of money from rich people who live in the country, and taking to all kinds of crime and violence. Why is it that the inhabitants do not band together and pursue these brigands, and bring them bound before the authorities, who would see that justice was done to them? It should be pointed out that there are already several of them in prison at Dijon, but their capture was due to the watchfulness and zeal of our magistrates and of the National Guard and gendarmerie, who are after all less concerned in the matter than those people who are likely to suffer personally and directly from the greed of these scoundrels. We hope the present information will have the desired effect.

News of the Department, 21 October 1815:

The prefect of the department was informed, on the 6th inst., that after a jollification held on the night of the 1st/2nd certain undesirable elements from the town of Seurre and its neighbourhood came out with cries of 'Long live Napoleon!' and 'Down with the royalists!' and caused a great scandal in the town. Having been informed that certain individuals who belonged to the partisan corps in the Côte d'Or three months ago, and were known for their brigandage in the neighbour-

GSF B

hood of Besançon, were the instigators of this disturbance, the prefect, after consulting the public prosecutor, ordered their arrest.... This arrest has produced excellent results. It has been approved by the majority of inhabitants, who realize that these constant threats to their peace come from a small number of malcontents who can only be brought to their senses by severe measures.

News of the Department, 6 December 1815:
We have received a letter from Montmoyen in the canton of Recey, arrondissement of Châtillon-sur-Seine, informing us that on Sunday last, at the end of Mass in the parish church, the mayor, accompanied by the municipal guard, read out the acts concerning general security and the repression of seditious cries, and then gave orders for tricoloured flags and sashes to be burnt in the public square. The mayor read out a proclamation in which he advised all who came under his jurisdiction to obey the law and be faithful to their king, and ended up with this noteworthy exhortation: 'Citizens, the colours of usurpation are banned for ever! Let us fling these signs of rebellion into the flames, and woe betide those who try to wear them or have them revived!'

News of the Department, 9 December 1815:
The Comte de Choiseul,[16] prefect, has just sent the mayors of the department of Côte d'Or a circular letter, dated 24 November, in which he informs them of the closing down of the examining board before which the soldiers returning home have been appearing, and explains very wisely the importance of this operation and the results that might be expected from it. In speaking of the soldiers who have been recalled to the colours, he writes, 'They no longer run the risk of fighting in distant and hazardous wars, which have caused French lives to be lost in countries to which no French interest could ever have called our soldiers. It is in their own country that they will serve, and in the real interests of their country that they will be armed.... If the return of the king had not put an end to wars which looked like going on for ever, hardly any of them would have seen their homes, parents and friends again. All would have died before their time. I would call your attention, equally forcibly, to the soldiers who have been discharged from the army. May they learn to appreciate the goodness of the king who, taking into account all their family circumstances, has

16 André Urbain Maxime de Choiseul D'Aillecourt (1782-1854) served Napoleon in a number of administrative posts, but rallied to the Bourbons in 1814 and became prefect of the Eure. Dismissed from this post during the Hundred days, he was appointed prefect of the Côte d'Or in July 1815.

increased the number of exemptions with real fatherly care. They must prove themselves worthy, by their conduct, of the favour they have received. . . . I shall keep a watchful eye on all retired soldiers, and at the slightest fault or the slightest murmur against the government I shall not hesitate to have their pensions taken away.'

Journal de la Côte d'Or, 12, 15, 19 July, 21 October, 6, 9 December, 1815

5   Repressive measures

Elections were held in August 1815 according to rules devised by the king. They produced a Chamber of Deputies dominated by zealous royalists, known thereafter as *ultras*. Not all the members of the 'Chambre Introuvable' (Incomparable Chamber) as Louis called it were embittered émigrés: on the contrary, more than half were of bourgeois origin: but they were determined to organize a judicial terror all over France. They claimed that their repressive measures, which included the suspension of individual liberty and the formation of provost courts, bore no resemblance to Jacobin dictatorship, but the distinction was not clear to contemporaries. English observers were especially critical of the following act, as displaying an excessive attention to detail.

An act for the repression of seditious cries and incitements to revolt, 9 November 1815

Article 1. The following persons shall be prosecuted and tried before a criminal court: All those guilty of having printed, displayed, distributed, sold or published writings, or of having uttered cries or delivered speeches in public squares or in any place normally used for public gatherings, whenever such cries, speeches or writings shall have threatened the life of the king or of any members of the royal family, whenever they shall have aroused feelings against royal authority or have provoked, either directly or indirectly, an attempt to overthrow the government or change the order of succession to the throne, even when such attempts have had no effect and have not been connected with any conspiracy. Those found guilty of the said offences shall be transported.

Article 2. The following shall be liable to the same penalty: all persons found guilty of having hoisted a flag other than the white flag in a public square or in any place normally used for public gatherings.

Article 3. The penalty of transportation shall be inflicted on all persons who utter seditious cries in the king's palace or along the route of a royal procession.

Article 4. The crimes specified in the preceding articles shall be tried in the assize courts.

Article 5. The following shall be regarded as seditious: all cries, all speeches delivered in public squares or in any place normally used for public gatherings, and all published writings, even those which, without having been printed, have been either displayed, sold, distributed, or handed in for printing, whenever, by means of these cries, speeches, or writings, an attempt shall have been made to weaken, by lies or insults, the respect due to the person or authority of the king, or to the person of any member of the royal family, or whenever such cries, speeches and writings shall have invoked the name of the usurper or of any member of his family, or of any other leader of rebellion, or have incited others to disobey the king and the constitutional charter.

Article 6. The following also shall be regarded as guilty of seditious acts: the authors, sellers, distributors or exhibitors of drawings or pictures, the making, exhibiting or distributing of which tends to the same purpose as the cries, speeches and writings mentioned in the preceding article.

Article 7. The following shall be regarded as seditious acts: the removal or defacing of the white flag, the arms of France, or other symbols of royal authority, and the manufacture, carrying or distribution of any other cockades or symbols of allegiance either prohibited or unauthorized by the king.

Article 8. The following shall be regarded as guilty of seditious acts: all persons who shall have spread or sanctioned alarm over the inviolability of property known as national land, or rumours of an alleged re-establishment of tithes or feudal rights, or news likely to alarm people as to the maintenance of lawful authority and thus shake their fidelity.

Article 9. The following also shall be regarded as seditious: speeches and writings as mentioned in article 5 of the present act, should they contain only indirect provocation to the offences specified in articles 5, 6, 7 and 8 of the present act, or cause it to be believed that offences of this nature, or of the nature described in articles 1, 2 and 3, will be committed, or give false information as to their having been committed.

Article 10. Authors and accomplices of the offences specified in articles 5, 6, 7, 8 and 9 of the present act shall be tried by the correctional police tribunals[17]; they shall be sentenced to terms of imprisonment ranging from a maximum of five years to a minimum of three years. They shall also be liable to a minimum fine of 50 francs, which may be increased to as much as 20,000 francs. Those who have been found guilty and are in receipt of a civilian or army retirement pension or of unemployment benefit shall be deprived of the whole or a part of such pension or benefit for such time as shall be determined by the court. Those sentenced shall also, after the expiry of their term of imprisonment, be kept under police observation for such time as shall be specified by the court, this not exceeding five years. . . . In the case of a second offence the penalty shall be doubled.

[No duration was specified for the act, though in debate ultra-royalists excused their policies by saying that their legislation was meant to be of a temporary nature. This act remained in force until repealed by the press legislation of May 1819.]

Bulletin des lois, 7ᵉ serie, tome premier, 1815, no. 39

[17] Trial in these courts was by a panel of judges, without jury.

II

MODIFIED FREEDOM

1 Moderate liberalism

After a bout of severity, Restoration governments moved towards greater freedom. From September 1816, when the king dissolved the Chambre Introuvable, to December 1821, when he appointed Villèle as his Prime Minister, Louis's idea was to rule with moderate ministers who, although they did not have a permanent and assured majority in the Chambers, could try to hold the balance between parties. Inside the Chamber of Deputies this initiative on the part of the king was approved by liberal politicians, who were afraid of complete ministerial responsibility to parliament because of its democratic and revolutionary connotations and who realized, in the early years, that parliamentary initiative might result in ultra-royalist government. The following is an extract from a speech in the Chamber by a revered liberal deputy.

Royer-Collard:[1] I do not think it is necessary for our ministers to have a permanent and assured majority as they have in England. Look at the difference between the component parts of the two systems of government. In England the initiative, which is the beginning of all business, along with the chief executive power and a large part of government rests with the House of Commons. With us the whole of government is in the hands of the king: he does not need the help of the Chambers unless he sees the necessity for a new law or for the budget. Now, in a country where so many laws have been made, the thought that there might be an irrefutable case for a new law is almost hypothetical, and if there *was* an absolute necessity for one there can be no doubt that the Chamber would pass it. As for the budget, this is no more the business of the king than it is of the Chamber; it is the business of the whole nation, because its entire existence depends upon it. The budget as presented by the minister can be amended – modified – in the interests

[1] Pierre Paul Royer-Collard (1763-1845) came of a wealthy Jansenist family. He was appointed professor of philosophy at the Sorbonne in 1811 and elected deputy for the Marne in 1815.

of the king and the state, but in the end a budget has to be adopted which conforms to the needs of the state, and one cannot imagine the existence of a Chamber which, in order to enforce its own views or its opposition to the government, would condemn the nation to death through the disruption or suspension of the public services. If such a situation ever did arise, the king would be within his rights in turning to the people, and he could be sure that they would help him to save the state.

I would go further and say that the day when the government only exists by the approval of the majority in the Chamber, the day when it is recognized as a fact that the Chamber can repudiate the king's ministers and make him take others which are not of his choosing but of its own, that day will see the end not only of the Chamber but of our monarchy – of that independent monarchy which protected our fathers and from which alone France has received all the liberty and good fortune she has ever known. On that day we would have a republic.

Archives parlementaires: Chambre des Députés,
12 February 1816

2 Popular liberalism

Outside the Chamber, liberals expressed dissatisfaction with a régime which fell far behind their ideals. One of the most popular journals of the time was the *Minerve*, a review founded in February 1818 and appearing more or less weekly but at irregular intervals in order to escape the police regulations laid down for periodicals by a law of 21 October 1814. Subscriptions soon rose to 10,000. According to police reports the most popular item was Etienne's *Letter from Paris*, in which information supplied by provincial correspondents was used to reveal administrative abuses.[2]

We [writers in the *Minerve*] are not enemies of the government, nor do we think we are altogether useless to it. . . . Either the ministers know about the abuses which exist, or they *don't* know. If the first, they need to be told that they are failing in their duty by not repressing them; if the second, they need to be enlightened by tearing away the veil which flattery has put between them and the truth. For my own part, I am pleased to say that I think they are deceived about the evils

[2] Charles Guillaume Etienne (1777-1845) had achieved some success as a playwright during the Empire and had been appointed censor to the *Journal de l'Empire*. He had been deprived of his literary honours as well as his job at the return of the Bourbons.

afflicting the country. I would go further and say that it is impossible for them always to be aware of them. A glance at the administration will show how this can come about. In each department their principal representative is the prefect. His activities are scrutinized by a general council, which alone has the right of expressing wishes and preferring complaints; but the members are nominated by the prefect. If there were independent mayors, these at least would be able to veto the mistakes he makes in his zeal or the arbitrary extensions he makes to his power; but the mayors too are nominated by him. The mayors in turn have duties to perform: they administer the property of the commune, they dispose of its funds, they have to protect the citizens and see to it that favours and responsibilities are equally distributed. If they abuse their power; if, from being the tutelary magistrates that they are, they become petty tyrants; who will be able to voice the complaints of the oppressed? Who will expose injustices, abuses, or malpractices? The town council, you will say. Ah! but the town council is also nominated by the prefect. Thus, any given department looks as though it has four hundred officials, but in fact it only has one: it is the prefect who administers, judges, spends, controls and confirms. The general council, which is composed of his own creatures, does nothing to upset his schemes; and, as though this official who can nominate all the overseers of his administration were not already strong enough, it was decided recently that he should be allowed to attend meetings of the council. . . .

It would be interesting to publish the minutes of most of these councils since 1815. One would think one were listening to men of the sixteenth century who had risen from the grave to discuss the affairs of the present day. A man who is in a position to know told me the other day that in one of these gothic assemblies there had been opposition to the allocation of funds for promoting vaccination, on the grounds that there was too great an increase in population already and that anything which tended to foster it was harmful. . . .

It is the same with the town councils as with the general councils; they are the most obedient servants of their honours the mayors. Almost everywhere the latter have packed them with their own bailiffs, farmers, caretakers and gamekeepers. How impartially rates are assessed! How well the accounts are examined! In some communes, property owners who could have stood up to the mayor have been removed from the council and replaced by the latter's own men. The village police are nominated by the mayor, and, as you can well imagine, they are not always chosen in the interests of a certain class of property owner. I have been told of a commune where all the chief

taxpayers met and requested that the position of constable be given to a
gallant ex-serviceman, but the mayor, who is churchwarden of the
parish and pays only 5 francs in taxes, gave preference to the verger.

So, the ministers nominate the prefects and the prefects nominate the
mayors; and the prefects and the mayors nominate the general councils
and the town councils to which they submit the budget for their departments and communes. The only thing missing is for the ministers
to nominate the deputies to whom they submit the budget for the state.
Extreme supporters of the ministry have this in the back of their minds,
for writers in their newspapers and prefects in their circulars would
certainly like us, when choosing men to examine the accounts rendered
by the ministers, to choose men chosen by the ministers. Add to this
state of affairs the right which prefects have of nominating juries, the
provisions of our penal code which leave individual liberty at the mercy
of any officer of the judicial police, the law which submits press offences
to the correctional police tribunals, the law which enslaves newspapers,
and the so-called 'transitory' law of 9 November 1815 which is still in
force in 1818; and tell me, please, if there was ever a nation less free,
with a Charter which guarantees freedom.

— *Minerve*, 12 September, 1818

3 Fear of revolution

In 1819 the government introduced freedom of the press. This was done just at a
time when popular agitation was coming to a head in many parts of Europe.
Ultra-royalists seized every opportunity to criticize the government for making
concessions to the Left at such a time. The following is a typical article from the
Quotidienne, a royalist daily newspaper founded in 1792, suppressed in 1797, and
revived in 1814 by its original editor, Michaud.

In England liberals hold meetings, in Germany they commit murder, in
France they write articles whilst waiting for something better. They
write to justify the murders committed by their brethren in Germany
and the meetings held by their brethren in London and Manchester.[3]
If the homicidal mania of the German students crossed the Rhine, if the
crowds rioted in our cities as they are doing in England, what would
become of the government? What would become of society? When
one asks oneself these questions, and sees the indifference of the ministry,

---

[3] This article was written after the murder of the journalist Kotzebue by a German
student on 23 March 1819 but before the 'massacre' of Peterloo on 16 August.

one cannot help feeling intensely alarmed. It is at times like these that we need faithful citizens, ready to sacrifice their lives to repress insurrection, to save the throne, and to maintain law and order. France used to have such generous citizens, known both for their devotion and for their military prowess. What has become of them? The ministry has got rid of them, as though to leave the field open for revolt.[4]. . . If disorder were to return, this country would have no defenders left. Presumably the ministers, who have brought us to this sorry pass, are relying on the devotion of their minions – men who would defend nothing, because they live for self. Does the ministry think that the men whom it has loaded with places, money, and favours would be any the more zealous on that account? Men who need to be paid to have their loyalty aroused back out in the hour of danger, because they think only of the day when they will no longer be paid.

Quotidienne, 31 July 1819

4 Liberal electioneering

Liberals won more and more seats in the annual elections which renewed a fifth of the Chamber. Here is a typical election manifesto from a Liberal candidate, sent to the Minister of the Interior by the prefect of Charente-Inférieure on 25 September 1819.

Ever since April 1814 I have been on half-pay,[5] and I have decided not to apply for active service unless France should be obliged to engage in a truly national war. I shall do all I can to obtain the guarantees that we now lack, such as the establishment of a jury system on foundations more in keeping with representative government, the establishment of elected municipal and departmental government, the organization of national guards, big reforms in the permanent army, a judicial system which is less costly, and the amendment of our penal code and of all laws, decrees, senatus-consulta and ordinances which are not in accordance with the Charter. I shall oppose the formation of entails and the reinstatement of guilds, and I shall demand true liberty of conscience.

In my opinion the government ought not to have anything to do

---

[4] A reference to recent dismissals of ultra-royalists from administrative posts at the instigation of Decazes, the Minister of the Interior.

[5] In April 1814, about 12,000 officers were put on half-pay and sent home. After some initial difficulties most of them found decent jobs and were able to live fairly comfortably, but liberals were always reminding them of their blighted military careers and suggesting that they had been ill-rewarded for their services to their country.

with religion except in a fatherly kind of way to maintain toleration between the different denominations. I distrust pious hypocrites who, while very often causing us unhappiness in this world, show too ardent a zeal for making us happy in the next. I believe that governments should have no other function than that of ensuring the safety of persons and property and of securing for everyone much greater freedom in their work and in the pleasures that result from it. Anything that they wish to do apart from this appears to me to be usurpation and despotism. A government that itself does the wrong that it is supposed to prevent; a government which mulcts people, or imprisons people unjustly, or hampers work by means of monopolies and customs barriers, or would like to impose its opinions on us and prevent us from expressing our own views, appears to me to be a barbarous government.

I regard revolutions as detrimental to civilization; I cannot imagine that a people which is incapable of controlling or reforming its government would be able to establish a better one by violence. The laws concerning elections and liberty of the press, if they are not spoilt, seem to me sufficient to safeguard our institutions and even improve them; provided, too, that we know how to use them. I believe that education ought not to be a monopoly in the hands of the government,[6] and that it has no right to fashion the generations according to its own designs, in the way that we breed domestic animals and train them for our purposes or our pleasure. I shall continue to support the method of mutual education,[7] as I have done over the past four years.

I believe that people are not by nature enemies of each other but that their dissensions stem from wicked governments. I consider customs barriers an evil imposed on mankind by those in authority, and it seems to me that civilisation ought gradually to be freed from these shackles which hinder and retard its progress.

Arch. nat. F⁷6740

5 Bonapartism

The most popular poet of the Restoration was Béranger.[8] His little poems voiced all the prejudices of the ordinary people: dislike of aristocrats and priests,

[6] Education throughout France was under the control of a governing body still popularly known by its Napoleonic name of 'the University'. From 1815 to 1820 this consisted of a commission of five members appointed by the king, officially called the Commission of Public Instruction.

[7] Teaching with the aid of monitors, as in the system devised by Bell and Lancaster in Britain.

[8] Pierre Jean de Béranger (1780–1857).

irreverence towards authority, and nostalgic memories of the comradeship of war. In December 1821 he was tried for libel. The trial created a tremendous sensation, the passages and doorways leading into the courtroom being so jammed with sightseers that the presiding judge had to enter through a window. Béranger was sentenced to three months imprisonment and 400 francs fine.

Marchangy, Public Prosecutor[9]:
It is one of the stratagems most familiar to factious writers, to try and impassion the memories of French soldiers by presenting peace as a disgrace and war as a right of which they have been unjustly deprived. No matter that these brave soldiers have nobly laid down their arms at a word from the father of their country, knowing that allegiance to him can alone make a virtue out of courage; no matter that they have been thankful, after the long exile to which victory condemned them, to return to the family roof and family affection. It is actually in the Elysian fields, where their valour rests, that the serpent of sedition tries to crawl among their laurels, besmirching them with its foul venom and sullying them with the breath of madness and error. Hearken to the nsinuations and hypocritical whinings that this spirit of temptation offers to these faithful warriors! To listen to it, these warriors are nothing but humiliated and degraded men. Because kingdoms are no longer thrown to them as prey, they are made to shed imaginary tears over the ill fate of France, who, instead of having the advantage of being depopulated by triumphs or ruined by reverses, enjoys today an unhoped for prosperity under the new yoke of the same Bourbons who have ruled us for centuries. Murderous compassion, that weeps at seeing Europe no longer devastated! Selfish devotion, that regrets seeing battlefields no longer transformed into arenas for ambiton and personal interest!

M. Béranger has attempted in twenty songs to pervert the military spirit in this way, notably in the song entitled:

The Old Flag[10]
My old companions in our days
Of glory greet me here;

---

[9] Louis Antoine François de Marchangy (1782-1826) was procureur to the tribunal of the Seine under both Napoleon and the Bourbons. He acquired a great reputation for eloquence, although he was incapable of improvising the merest sentence. He reached his greatest fame with his pitiless accusation of the Four Sergeants of La Rochelle in 1822. When elected to the Chamber in 1823 he voted with the extreme right.

[10] The metrical translation is taken from W. Young, *Béranger: Two Hundred of his Lyrical Poems done into English Verse* (New York, 1850).

Drunk with remembrances, the wine
    Hath made my memory clear:
Proud of my own exploits and theirs,
My flag my straw-thatched cottage shares.
      Ah! when shall I shake off the dust
      In which its noble colours rust?

Beneath the straw where, poor and maimed,
    I sleep, 'tis hid from view:
That flag for twenty years from fight
    To fight triumphant flew;
And decked with laurels and with flowers
Blazed forth before all Europe's powers.
      Ah! when . . . etc.

All, all our blood that it hath cost
    This flag repaid to France;
Our sons, on Liberty's broad breast,
    Have sported with its lance:
Let it once more make tyrants own
That Glory is plebeian grown!
      Ah! when . . . etc.

Its eagle is laid low, worn out
    By many a distant deed:
Up with the Gallic cock! – that too
    The thunderbolt could speed!
France shall forget her late distress
And, proud and free, that emblem bless.
      Ah! when . . . etc.

    . . . .

But it is here, beside my arms;
    One glance I'll dare bestow;
Come forth, my flag! my hope! and bid
    My tears no longer flow.
When tears bedew the warrior's eye,
In pity Heaven shall hear their cry;
      Yes! yes! I will shake off the dust
      In which thy noble colours rust!

After hearing verses like that, I ask you if what we have here is really
the light and gay song for which indulgence is craved. The author calls

this piece a song: he puts it to the tune of 'She loves to laugh, she loves to drink'. But none of that can destroy its shady and hostile character. You must ask yourself in what circumstances it could be sung without becoming a manifesto and an insult. At a military banquet, perhaps? In barracks? On the march? In town or country? It could not be sung except by a band of conspirators, and to serve as a signal for rebellion. That is its purpose! That is the real reason why it was written!

Procès fait aux chansons de P. J. Béranger (Paris, 1821) pp. 15-29

III

ULTRA-ROYALIST GOVERNMENT

1 The Law of the Double Vote, 29 June 1820

By 1819 ministers were alarmed at the number and character of left-wing deputies elected to the Chamber. They were already planning to modify the electoral system when the assassination of the Duc de Berry on 13 February 1820 led to a public outcry against the Left and obliged them to introduce a more drastic measure. The law of the Double Vote gave overwhelming success to ultra-royalists in the partial elections of 1820 and 1821. In December 1821 the king appointed an ultra-royalist ministry under the Comte de Villèle.

Article 1. There shall be in each department an electoral college for the department and electoral colleges for the arrondissements. . . .

Article 2. The departmental colleges shall be composed of electors who pay the most taxes, in number equalling one quarter of the total number of electors in the department. The departmental colleges shall elect 172 new deputies, in accordance with the table appended to this law. [The table has been omitted from this extract.] They shall proceed with this election for the session 1820. The election of the 258 existing deputies is assigned to the arrondissement colleges to be formed in each department in accordance with article 1. . . . Each of these arrondissement colleges shall elect one deputy. . . .

Article 6. To proceed to the election of the deputies, each elector shall write down his vote secretly at the polling booth, or have it written down for him by another elector of his own choice, on a ballot paper received for the purpose from the president; he shall hand his ballot paper, completed and folded, to the president, who shall put it into the ballot box provided for the purpose. . . .

L. Duguit and H. Monnier, *op. cit.*, pp. 387-8

2   The Law of Tendency, 17 March 1822

Villèle could not re-introduce censorship for newspapers, for the liberal press law of 1819 had made it clear that censorship was contrary to the Charter. Instead he introduced novel elements into the law of libel. For a time journalists were thoroughly subdued by the thought of these measures, and it was not until a leading liberal newspaper was acquitted on charges brought under the new law in December 1825 that they took heart.

Article 1. No newspaper or periodical, devoted wholly or partly to news or political matter, and appearing either regularly on certain days or in separate numbers at irregular intervals, shall be founded and published without the king's consent. ·

Article 2. The first copy of each paper or the first number of each periodical or magazine shall be deposited as soon as it is printed at the local office of the public prosecutor.

Article 3. If the character of a newspaper or periodical, emerging from a series of articles, shall have a tendency to endanger law and order, or the respect due to the state religion or other religions recognized in France, or the authority of the king, or the stability of constitutional government or the inviolability of sales of national land and the undisturbed possession of these properties, the royal courts shall, each in its own area, in a solemn session of two chambers, and after hearing the public prosecutor and the parties concerned, pronounce suspension of the newspaper or political journal for a period not exceeding one month for the first offence and three months for the second. After two of these suspensions, and in the event of a repetition of the offence, total suppression may be ordered.

Bulletin des lois, 7ᵉ série, tome 14ᵉ, 1822, no. 510

3   Intervention in Spain

Ever since revolt broke out in Spain in 1820, vociferous sections of the ultra-royalist party had been insisting that France should intervene to restore the authority of Ferdinand VII. Villèle was against intervention, but pressure from within the party, and especially from the Foreign Secretary Chateaubriand, obliged him to give in. A French expeditionary force under the Duc d'Angoulême crossed the frontier on 7 April 1823 and entered Madrid without resistance on 24 May.

Chateaubriand[1]: Let us first examine the question of intervention. No government has the right to interfere in the affairs of another nation unless the immediate safety and vital interests of that government are endangered. The exception, gentlemen, appears to me to be as incontestable as the rule: no state can allow its vital interests to perish without perishing itself as a state. . . . It must be proved now that this exception to the rule applies to us, and that our vital interests are being impaired.

First of all, our vital interests are impaired by the fact that the Spanish revolution is holding up a part of our commerce. We are obliged to keep warships in American waters, which are infested with pirates engendered by the anarchy in Spain. Several of our merchant ships have been pillaged, and we have not, like Britain, the naval forces at our disposal to compel the Cortes to compensate us for our losses.

For another thing, it is a matter of the greatest urgency to our provinces bordering on Spain that order should be restored on the other side of the Pyrenees. As far back as June 1820, when there was no question of war, an honourable member stated from this rostrum that the Spanish revolution, by interrupting communications with France, was reducing the value of land in the department of Landes by a half. The trade in mules and pack-horses alone, he said, was of considerable value: the peasants of Rouergue, Haute-Auvergne, Haut Limousin and Poitou often paid their land tax with the money they received from the sale of pack horses, and it was not until one got beyond Dauphiné that this advantageous trade stopped. Our corn from the south also found its way into Spain, where it was paid for in piastres, further profit being made on the exchange. Our cloth, too, found a vast market in the ports of the Spanish peninsula; the disturbances that followed the military revolt on the Isle of Léon considerably reduced this trade, and any government would be reprehensible which allowed a whole population to be ruined without protecting it. Are people hoping that the civil wars will come to an end and leave the way free for our trade? Don't count on it: nothing comes to an end of its own accord in Spain, neither passions nor virtues.

Our consuls threatened, our ships driven away from Spanish ports, our territory violated three times – does not this mean that our vital interests are endangered? . . . Our territory violated! What for? To go and cut the throats of a few wretched wounded soldiers from the royalist army, who had thought to die in peace in the arms, as it were,

---

[1] François René, Vicomte de Chateaubriand (1768-1848), the famous writer, was appointed Secretary of State for Foreign Affairs in place of the Duc de Montmorency in November 1822.

of our generous motherland. Our peasants heard their cries, and in their cottages they blessed the king to whom they owed the good fortune of being delivered from revolutions.

Our vital interests are further compromised by the mere fact of having to keep an army of observation on the frontiers of Spain. How many days, months, years will we have to maintain this army? This state of semi-hostility has all the disadvantages of war without any of its advantages: it weighs upon our finances, worries public opinion, and exposes the soldiers, who have been inactive for too long, to all the corrupting influences of agents of discord. Why was the army of observation established? . . . [Here Chateaubriand read a note from the Duke of Wellington describing the army of observation as established, justifiably, by France to protect herself against moral contagion.] Moral contagion! The words are not mine, gentlemen, but I hereby declare that I too regard moral contagion as the most frightening aspect of all. It is this above all which endangers our vital interests. Who does not know that Spain's revolutionaries are in correspondence with our own? Have they not publicly tried to incite our soldiers to revolt? Have they not threatened us that they would carry the tricolour flag down from the heights of the Pyrenees to bring back the son of Bonaparte? . . . People say that this revolution is isolated, confined to the Peninsula whence it cannot spread. As if, in the state of civilisation that the world has reached, there were any states in Europe that were strangers to each other! . . .

I come now, gentlemen, to the great question of the Alliance and the Congress.[2] The Alliance has been dreamed up for the enslavement of the world; tyrants have gathered together to conspire against the nations; at Verona France begged the help of Europe to destroy liberty; at Verona our plenipotentiaries compromised the honour and sold the independence of their country; at Verona the military occupation of Spain and France was agreed upon. Cossacks are hurrying from their distant haunts to execute the commands of kings, forcing France to take part in a hateful war, as in ancient times the slaves were sometimes forced to march into battle. (Laughter from the Right.) It is at this point, gentlemen, that I am obliged to make an effort of self control, to

---

[2] On 20 November 1815, Britain, Russia, Austria and Prussia signed a Quadruple Alliance, designed to deal with any further trouble from France. In 1818 the alliance was renewed secretly, whilst openly France was admitted to a Quintuple Alliance of the Great Powers. In the eyes of liberals this associated her too closely with her old enemy Britain and with the three reactionary states of Russia, Austria and Prussia, popularly known as the 'Holy Alliance Powers'. Representatives of all five countries met at a Congress at Verona in the autumn of 1822 to discuss policy towards Spain.

reply with the detachment and moderation that dignity of character demand. It is difficult, I must confess, to hear unmoved these strange accusations brought against a former minister, who commands the respect of all who come into contact with him.[3] . . . As for my noble colleagues at the Congress of Verona, it would be an insult to defend them. A companion of the king in exile,[4] a friend of the Duc de Berry,[5] are above the suspicion of having betrayed their country's interests. There remains only myself. The Chamber does not need apologies from me, but I venture to say that among so many honourable members there is not one that I look upon as a better Frenchmen than myself. (Great excitement.)

Gentlemen, I must make a confession. I arrived at the Congress with prejudices that were far from favourable to it. . . . But what was I forced to see at Verona? Princes full of moderation and justice; upright kings whose subjects would willingly have called them friends if they had not had them as masters. . . . At Verona the principle adhered to was that of peace. At Verona the allied powers never spoke of waging war on their own account against Spain, but they believed that France, whose position was different, might be forced into war. Did this conviction result in the birth of treaties burdensome and dishonourable to France? No. Was there ever, even, a question of allowing foreign troops to pass through French territory? No, never. What then? It happened that because France is one of five great powers forming an alliance, an alliance to which she will always adhere and which already goes back eight years, she will in certain well-defined circumstances receive support which, far from affecting her dignity, will confirm the high status she holds in Europe.[6] (Laughter from the Left. Shouts from the Right: Bravo! etc.)

[3] Matthieu, Duc de Montmorency (1767-1826), France's foreign secretary in 1822 and her leading plenipotentiary at Verona, virtually committed France to act in Spain as the agent of the Alliance, i.e. of Russia, Austria and Prussia, since Britain dissociated herself from intervention. Montmorency was known to hold extreme royalist views, and the Left spread the rumour that he had invited foreign despots to help France crush liberty in Spain then destroy her own parliamentary institutions. He was assisted at the Congress by Chateaubriand, Caraman and La Ferronays.

[4] Victor Louis Charles de Riquet, Duc de Caraman (1762-1839) had emigrated during the Revolution and was appointed ambassador to Russia in 1815.

[5] Pierre Louis Auguste Ferron, Comte de la Ferronays (1777-1842), also an émigré, was appointed ambassador to St. Petersburg in 1819.

[6] The three Eastern European powers agreed that France would have a right to go to war against Spain if she were attacked, or directly provoked by Spanish agents, or if the Spanish royal family and its rights of succession were threatened. Russia promised armed support, and Austria and Russia offered moral support. Britain dissociated herself from both promises.

France does not mean to impose institutions on Spain, gentlemen. . . . The Spaniards know what is best for themselves at this stage in their civilization. But I wish with all my heart for this great people liberty consistent with their principles, and institutions which will protect their virtues from the fickleness of fortune and the waywardness of men. Spaniards, you owe both your misfortune and your glory to France. She sent you her two plagues, Bonaparte and Revolution: deliver yourselves from the second as you did from the first!

With your permission, gentlemen, I should like to correct the comparison that has been suggested between the invasion by Bonaparte and that into which France is forced today; between a Bourbon who marches to the rescue of a Bourbon, and the usurper who came to take the crown of a Bourbon after he had laid hands on his person by unparalleled treachery; between a conqueror who marched in, destroying altars, killing monks and nuns, deporting priests, and overthrowing the country's institutions, and a grandson of St. Louis who comes to protect all that is sacred amongst men and who, banished once himself, comes to put an end to all banishments. Buonaparte could not find friends among the subjects of a Bourbon and the descendants of the hero of Castile. But *we* have neither assassinated the last of the Condés nor aroused El Cid, and the men who armed themselves against Buonaparte will fight for us.

. . . We must never forget that if war with Spain, like all wars, has its drawbacks and dangers, it will have had one immense advantage. It will have given us an army, it will have re-instated us as a military power among the nations, and it will have established our freedom and confirmed our independence. If there has been anything still lacking to complete the reconciliation of Frenchmen, it will be supplied on the battlefield. Brothers in arms soon become friends, and the past is forgotten at the thought of a common glory. The king – this king who is so wise, so fatherly, so peace-loving – has spoken. He has decided that the safety of France and the dignity of his crown make it his duty to resort to arms after negotiations have failed. The king has desired 100,000 soldiers to assemble under the orders of a prince who, at the crossing of the Drôme, showed himself to be as valiant as Henri IV.[7] The king, generously and confidently, has given the white flag into the safe keeping of captains who caused other colours to triumph. They will

[7] This is a reference to Angoulême's exploits during the Hundred Days. On hearing of the escape of Napoleon from Elba, Angoulême collected 10,000 troops in the royalist region around Nîmes and marched upon Lyon. He overcame resistance from National Guards at Montélimar, on the river Drôme, but Bonapartists captured Nîmes and forced him to retreat. He was taken prisoner on 16 April 1815.

teach it again the road to victory: it has never forgotten the path of honour.

> *Arch. parl,. Chambre des Députés,* 25 February
> 1823

4   The liberal viewpoint

The loyalty of the French army and its success in Spain discomposed French liberals and brought a temporary popularity to the ultra-royalist government. Villèle seized the opportunity for an electoral coup. The Chamber was dissolved on 24 December 1823 and elections ordered for some two months ahead, allowing time for pressure to be brought upon electors and a programme of legislation to be announced. The following extract from a liberal daily newspaper the *Constitutionnel* shows how liberals saw the situation.

Ever since the Charter came into existence there have been some men in France who wanted either to destroy it or turn it to their advantage. The dissolution of the Chamber, and the complete renewal which must follow, looks to them like a favourable opportunity.

To restore administrative duties to the clergy, and thereby transform a purely spiritual ministry into a political force which might interfere with citizens in their most important transactions and place illegal conditions upon the celebration of marriage, the legitimacy of children, and the last rites to the dead;

To invest the clergy with inalienable property, whilst top-rank civil servants draw salaries from the state;

To entrust them with the education of youth, and in so doing make the whole of the rising generation dependent on them for their future careers;

To hamper industry by the re-establishment of crippling guilds and vexatious masters;

To deprive industry of her influence in politics by brushing aside, on countless pretexts, electors who qualify by means of the patents tax, and concentrating electoral rights as far as possible in the hands of wealthy landowners;

To re-establish religious communities, contrary to the spirit and letter of the Charter, and to enrich them at the expense of private families;

To introduce another means of despoiling these same families by attacking equality of inheritance and creating a latent hostility between younger sons and the eldest;

To saddle the Treasury with the task of finding thirty millions in government bonds for the émigrés;

To oppose the division of property, which has been a source of prosperity for the citizen and of security for the throne;

In a word, to create a vast landowning aristocracy, and to achieve in France by legislation what has come about in England by abuse;

This is what these men are after; this is what they want.

Constitutionnel, 7 January 1824

5   The Septennial Act, 9 June 1824

Villèle was so pleased with the results of the elections, which reduced the liberal opposition in the Chamber of Deputies to 19, that he determined to make the Chamber last as long as possible without change.

Article 1. The present Chamber of Deputies and all those which come after it shall be re-elected as a whole. Unless previously dissolved by the king they shall last for seven years, counting from the day when the decree for their first meeting was issued.

L. Duguit and H. Monnier, *op. cit.*, p. 388

6   A change of monarch

On 16 September 1824 Louis XVIII died and was succeeded by his brother, the Comte d'Artois, as Charles X. Charles was known to be a religious bigot and was believed to hold reactionary political views. The following extract is translated from a letter – one of a long series – written by Thiers[8] to a German newspaper editor, Baron Cotta, for publication in the *Gazette d'Augsbourg*. The letter was never in fact published in the *Gazette*, either because Cotta found it distasteful or because he feared it would be censored. Thiers had begun his career as a lawyer at Marseilles. Arriving in Paris in 1821, he got a job on the editorial staff of the *Constitutionnel*. Rising at 5 a.m. daily, he devoted his mornings to the study of history and to writing articles for a variety of newspapers before going to the *Constitutionnel* in the afternoon.

Paris, 15 September 1824

The king has been dying since Sunday evening and it is now Wednesday. His excellent constitution is resisting death as it has stood up to his many infirmities in the past. The court has made no attempt to hide

[8] Marie Joseph Louis Adolphe Thiers (1797-1877).

his condition, and indeed has had no reason to keep it secret, being only too glad that an event like this should have taken place at a time when everything is calm and nothing is likely to happen to complicate the situation. Since Sunday evening, daily bulletins have been sent to the newspapers, couched in such a way as to leave no doubt about his impending death. Paris has remained perfectly calm. A vast crowd immediately gathered at the Tuileries and people crowded around the doorways to see the bulletins, not because they felt any sorrow but out of curiosity. I am not trying to distort the facts, because the courage with which the king is enduring his long drawn out agony, and the prospect of the reign which is to follow, have inspired me, along with many other men who share my opinions, with a sympathy that I never felt for him before. For all that, I can say that not one expression of sorrow has been uttered. The curiosity with which people go to the door and ask if the king is dead has, in its very naiveté, something shocking about it. It is as if people were at a theatre waiting for the curtain to rise and shouting 'Begin!' People in this country have not seen a king die in his bed for fifty years, and they have not seen a single important event for ten years. They are feeling, therefore, a strange need of emotion and novelty.

The king has shown extraordinary calm and courage throughout his illness. He seems to have taken a pride in dying a good death, which shows strength of character in itself, for it takes strength to preserve one's pride to the last. On Sunday, even, the day when his illness entered its last phase, he wanted to receive people. He insisted on reading his correspondence himself. He read two letters, very clearly. When he got to the second he paused and said to one of his attendants: 'Look! Here is a letter from an old and faithful servant who did a great deal to cheer us up during the long period of our misfortunes.' He then quoted some verses that this individual had written at the time when they were émigrés, repeating them with astonishing accuracy. Soon afterwards he dozed off and sank into the state of coma which he is in now. . . .

It is now fully agreed in Paris that his death will not have any serious repercussions and that we shall pass from Louis XVIII to Charles X or Philippe VII[9] without the slightest disturbance. The Comte d'Artois is telling everybody until he's blue in the face that nothing will be changed; that he intends to follow the same policy and put his trust in the same men as his brother. Nobody believes him, and the zealots show by their joy and the moderates by their fear that they have no

[9] A peculiar reference to Louis Philippe, Duc d'Orleans, who became Louis Philippe I in 1830.

confidence in the new ruler's promises. The Comte d'Artois is the weakest man in this degenerate family, well-known as it is for its weakness. At the same time he is a religious bigot, and he will very easily be led astray. No doubt he is in good faith when he promises to maintain the status quo, but in a few days he will be induced to change his mind and his plans. For the moment, however, it seems as though everything will be kept as it is. Apparently M. de Villèle has made complete arrangements for his own transfer. The need for money is the motive which will keep him in office under the new régime, they say. One cannot be sure of anything in the days to come, though. The fact is everyone is expecting the reign of the priests. On all sides one is told, 'The clerics are in!' The ultras make no attempt to hide their satisfaction. They evince notorious glee all around, and appear to flatter themselves that their long wait is at last ending, and about to give way to enjoyment of all the good things they have been longing for.

R. Marquand, *Thiers et le baron Cotta* (Paris, 1959) pp. 174-6

7   Indemnification of the émigrés

Villèle knew that the ultras could never become a conservative party like the English until landowners were united behind them. His scheme to give monetary compensation for land confiscated by the state during the Revolution was designed to cure the émigrés of a legitimate grievance and rid the owners of the land of a feeling of insecurity. The Minister of State, Martignac, introduced the bill in conciliatory terms, designed to associate the measure with the now popular Louis XVIII rather than with his distrusted successor. Unfortunately a bill had already been presented in 1824 attempting to obtain money for the indemnity by converting the interest on the national debt, and this enabled liberal newspapers to present the whole project as a plot to take wealth from middle-class bondholders and bestow it upon the aristocracy. By the time the indemnity bill became law, it had been thoroughly blackened in the eyes of the public.

Martignac[10]: As you know, gentlemen, during that period of unhappy memory when our royal family was separated from the land of France, men were very uncertain and divided in their opinion as to what they

---

[10] Jean Baptiste Sylvère Gaye, Vicomte de Martignac (1778-1832) was recognized as one of the most eloquent speakers in the Chamber. He had been devoted to the royal family since his encounter with the Duchesse d'Angoulême in her flight from Napoleon during the Hundred Days. He accompanied Angoulême to Spain in 1823 and was made Minister of State on his return.

ought to do. Some thought that it was wise, in the interests of the throne and of the country, to remain on the scarred but beloved soil of the fatherland: others believed that honour and loyalty obliged them to follow their unfortunate prince to that foreign land where he had sought asylum. A large number of Frenchmen, therefore, left their native country, which was already threatened with all the evils that follow in the wake of anarchy.

Heaven forbid that we should retrace here the sinister events that marked that period of trouble and disorder. Every effort must be made to destroy the memory of them! I shall recall only such evils as we are obliged in the name of wisdom and justice to redress, and which it would be folly and injustice to forget.

Harsh and threatening laws summoned back to France those people who had fled. Their refusal to return, though perfectly understandable now, called down on their heads laws of fury and vengeance – exile for life, or sentence of death. These laws were not enough. a means was sought to strike at both the absentees and their families. The spirit of hatred found it: their property was first of all sequestered, then confiscated, then put up for sale. . . .

Several years passed by. When circumstances had changed the position of the émigrés and they were permitted to see France again, a considerable number came back, and some of them obtained restitution of such of their property as remained in the hands of the state. Things were at this stage when Louis XVIII regained the throne of his ancestors. There can be no doubt that one of the immediate desires of his heart was to help those whose noble suffering was bound up with his own misfortunes, but the immediate dictates of his wisdom were to secure public tranquillity in the kingdom that had been restored to him. Twenty-five years had passed over France, and the deep marks left by their passing were encountered at every step. . . . Soon new evils began to assail France. The costs of a long occupation were added to existing burdens. The king and the whole of France went all out once more to pay them off. . . . Then, when reserves were in hand and Louis XVIII was on the point of proposing to the Chambers the means of securing a general reconciliation with an act of reparation, the perils which menaced the king of Spain and the safety of our frontiers imposed new sacrifices upon us. . . . You will remember, gentlemen, how at the opening of last session that noble and beneficent king, whose fatherly voice you hear no more, expressed to you his desire to heal the last wounds of the Revolution. . . . The moment has at last arrived when this desire can be fulfilled. . . .

Of all the rights which society promises and must conserve, the right of property is without doubt the most sacred and the one to which the guarantee of law is most firmly attached. Of all the penalties which the law can pronounce and civil justice administer, the most cruel is the confiscation of a person's goods and chattels: an odious punishment which strikes at the condemned man through his descendants and allows the State to enrich itself with the spoils of those whom it has orphaned. In 1799 this penalty was abolished by solemn decree, in the name of justice and humanity: a few months later it was re-established in the name of vengeance and hatred. And how was it done? By a general measure involving all the families of those whom duty and danger had forced to flee the country. . . .

These dreadful laws have now disappeared; judicial confiscation itself has been effaced from our penal·codes. The king abolished it on his return, and in his enlightened wisdom which fought in advance against the errors of the future he declared that it could never be re-established. . . . [But] innumerable business transactions took place under the aegis of those laws that are now abolished. The sovereign peacemaker, in his wisdom, honoured them. The Charter, which has given these transactions the support of sovereign authority and legality, has declared them inviolable. Complete respect, deep and unreserved, must be given to that august sanction. . . . Yet there is in all conscience something stronger than the laws themselves, which advises that the State, in whose name these confiscations and sales were made – that the State, which received the money and has enjoyed it for thirty years – owes compensation to those who were thus violently dispossessed.

Several voices have been raised in opposition to this much-needed act of reparation. People have asked why the losses incurred by emigration should be the only ones for which compensation should be regarded as necessary. It is true that the Revolution produced evil of all kinds, and that misfortunes are found wherever one sees the traces of its fury and folly. It is true that we must give up the idea of curing all these different evils. The riches of France even now, when she has returned to a state of law and order, would not be sufficient to restore the losses sustained by France when she was impoverished by anarchy and licence. But if amongst the evils caused by the Revolution there is one that can rightly be singled out as the most serious and hateful, and reasonably called the most disastrous; if there is one whose origin constitutes an attack on the most sacred rights and whose effects are a constant source of division and hatred; ought we to be deterred from remedying that one evil, when it is in our power to do so, by the fact that we cannot cure all the others?

The émigrés lost everything all at once. All the evils which befell France struck them, and in addition they suffered still graver misfortunes which were reserved for them alone. Holders of government bonds were criminally let down and lost two thirds of their capital, but at least they preserved a part of it, and the fatal measure which deprived them of the one part left their other possessions intact. Price controls and paper money acted to the detriment of business men and financiers by altering and destroying their liquid assets, but they had no effect on their landed property. Those who suffered the evils of war saw their fields and homesteads devastated, but at least the soil remained to them. The laws against the émigrés took everything – their shares, their goods, their income; and in addition these cruel laws deprived them, and them alone, of their fields, of their houses, of that part of their native soil for the preservation of which the owner has the right to demand protection and security from society.

It is for this latter misfortune that reparation is demanded. It is a misfortune quite out of the common run; nothing else can be compared with it. . . . If it were not so on account of the extent of the loss, gentlemen, it would be so on account of its origin and nature. The act that despoiled them was not the sort of confiscation that the criminal laws used to prescribe against some particular crime. . . . The confiscation launched against the émigrés was not an established penalty but a studied vengeance. It was wholesale confiscation, the sort of confiscation that follows on proscriptions. . . . Violent laws like that, laws of anger which strike either at the existence or at the property of a whole mass of citizens, are disasters which shake the very foundations of society. . . . It is important that a notable precedent should indicate once and for all that grave injustice must with time receive great amends. It is up to France to set this precedent. It must be done frankly and loyally, under the aegis of a king who is the protector of all rights and under the influence of an eminently conservative Charter, as an additional pledge, a new guarantee.

But this is not all. There are motives of another nature which indicate quite clearly that the evils we are preparing to remedy cannot be classed with others, and that it is a matter of the deepest concern to everybody that they should be remedied. . . . Notwithstanding the genuine security which has been and must continue to be given to the new owners, notwithstanding the irrevocable guarantee accorded to their titles, it must be admitted that public opinion persists in maintaining distinctions which the law has effaced. Land confiscated from the émigrés does not easily find purchasers, and its market value is nothing in proportion to its real value. Only compensation allotted to the former owners can bring the language of the Charter home to everybody: only compensation can eliminate the difference which still exists between proprietors of the same soil. The proposed reparation will in this way benefit the State, by putting back into profitable circulation funds that have become sterile. It will benefit it even more by strengthening unity and peace, the primary source of all prosperity.

Arch. parl., *Chambre des Députés*, 3 January 1825

IV

RELIGIOUS DISPUTES

1 The law against sacrilege

In 1825 Villèle submitted to the wishes of Charles X and a large section of the ultra-royalist party and introduced a bill for the punishment of sacrilege. The ostensible object was to diminish the number of thefts of sacred vessels from churches, but the real intention of the supporters of the bill was to strike a blow at the subordination of the church to the state, enshrined in Napoleon's Concordat. Liberal fears regarding the onset of reactionary policies under the cloak of religion were expressed by Royer-Collard, whose remarkable speech typified the high level of debate frequently attained during the Restoration. The bill passed but was never put into effect.

Royer-Collard: Gentlemen, the bill here presented to you is of a peculiar nature and one hitherto foreign to your deliberations. Not only does it introduce a new crime into your legislation, but, what is more extraordinary, it creates a new concept of criminality; a form of crime which is, as it were, supernatural, which falls outside the range of our experience, which human reason cannot discern or comprehend, and which manifests itself only to religious faith enlightened by revelation. . . .

The question concerns the crime of sacrilege. What is sacrilege? According to the bill it is the profaning of the sacred vessels and the consecrated host. What is profanation? It is any act of violence committed wilfully out of contempt and hatred for religion. . . . What is the consecrated host? We catholics believe – indeed we know by faith – that the consecrated host is no longer the host as we see it but Jesus Christ, the holiest of the holy, God and Man in one person, visible and invisible in the most awesome of our mysteries. Thus the act of violence is committed against Jesus Christ Himself. . . .

In substituting Jesus Christ, Son of God, Very God, for the consecrated host, what I have tried to do, gentlemen, is to establish by the irrefutable evidence of the bill itself, first, that the crime to be punished under the name of sacrilege is direct outrage upon the divine majesty, and second, that this crime arises entirely out of the catholic dogma of the Real Presence; so much so that if in your minds you separate the host from the presence of Jesus Christ and His divinity the sacrilege disappears along with the penalty inflicted upon it. It is the dogma which makes the crime. . . .

The question which arises goes far beyond that of freedom of worship. It is a question of knowing whether, in matters of religion, reason and conscience are answerable to God or to men: in other words, whether divine law is part of human law. It remains only for me to say that this is an atheistic question. . . . Gentlemen, human societies are born, and live, and die on earth. It is there that they accomplish their destiny; there that their imperfect and faulty justice, founded only on their own need and right of self-preservation, comes to an end. But society does not embrace the whole of man. After he has committed himself to society there remains to him the most noble part of himself – those lofty faculties by which he raises himself to God, to a future life, to wealth unknown in a world invisible. I refer to his religious beliefs, which constitute the grandeur of man, a charm against weakness and misfortune, a sure refuge against tyranny here below. Human law, relegated for ever to earthly things, has nothing to do with religious beliefs. In its temporal capacity it has no cognisance or comprehension of them; outside the concerns of this life it is fraught with ignorance and powerlessness. As religion is not of this world, so human law is not of the world beyond. The two worlds are joined but can never be confused. The grave is their boundary. . . .

I know very well that governments have a great interest in allying themselves with religion because it makes men better and therefore renders powerful assistance in the cause of order, peace, and the well-being of society. But such an alliance can only include the external and visible aspects of religion, its forms of worship and the position of its ministers within the state. Truth does not enter into it; truth falls neither within the power nor under the protection of men. . . .

And now, gentlemen, let us rise to an even higher plane. . . . A village of the Samaritans once refused to receive Jesus; and James and John, his disciples, said to him, 'Lord, wilt thou that we command fire to come down from heaven and consume them?' But he turned and rebuked them, saying, 'Ye know not what manner of spirit ye are of. The Son of Man is not come to destroy men's lives but to save them.' That, gentlemen, is the vocation of the Church; it has been called by Jesus Christ to save men, not consume them with fire from heaven. This explains the system of its penitential code: wholly medicinal, as

St Augustine says, and wholly occupied with destroying not men but sin, so that the sinner may be saved from eternal punishment, which is without cure. Over and above this code there lives and reigns the dogma of an afterlife, where God manifests his justice, which he hides and withholds in this life. This dogma is, in fact, at the heart of religious policy, and it opposes irrevocably the hasty infliction of punishment. I have proved that if one places religion within the scope of human law one denies the whole truth of religion: I now prove that if one places capital punishment within the scope of religion one denies the existence of an afterlife. The proposed law, which does both these things, is hence both ungodly and materialistic. It does not believe in the afterlife, this law which anticipates hell and fulfills on earth the function of the demons.[1]. . .

Here I lay aside the burden of this terrible discussion. I would not have ventured to take it up if I had consulted my own strength alone; but a profound conviction, and the feeling of a great duty to be fulfilled, have inspired and sustained me in my weakness. In breaking a long silence I wished to record my intense opposition to the system of theocracy which is threatening both religion and society, and which is so much more hateful because it is not, as in the days of barbarism and ignorance, the genuine fury of fanatical zeal which lights this torch. The theocracy of our times is less religious than political; it forms part of that system of universal reaction which is carrying us away; the thing which recommends it is that it is an aspect of the counter-revolution. It is true, gentlemen, that the Revolution was ungodly to the point of fanaticism, to the point of cruelty. But let this be a warning. It was that crime above all others which destroyed it. One can predict for the counter-revolution that reprisals for cruelty, even if they are no more than written, will bear witness against it and blight it in its turn.

                    Arch. parl., *Chambre des Députés*, 12 April 1825

2 The affair of the Constitutionnel

(a) *The newspaper articles in question*

The *Constitutionnel* cashed in on the religious zeal of the ultra-royalists by encouraging the anti-clerical sentiments of their opponents. In a series of small articles, no one of which was incriminating by itself, the editors tried to create the impression that there was a vast pseudo-religious conspiracy to destroy

---

[1] Royer-Collard was speaking in the debate on the first section of the bill, which prescribed capital punishment for sacrilege.

liberty. Police reported the *Constitutionnel* to be the most popular newspaper of the times, with a circulation of 18,000.

One of our subscribers who witnessed a mission in one of the departments in the north has sent us a booklet, printed at Lyon and issued with the approval of two Vicars-general, for distribution solely by missionaries.[2] Copies of this booklet, which is entitled *Self examination, Rule of Conduct, Remedies against Sin, Summary of the Faith*, have been sent to all the young people at boarding schools who played a full part in the mission. Designed for schoolchildren of both sexes, it is meant to serve as a guide in the self-examination which precedes confession. We opened this work with a feeling of respect, hoping to find in it a source of edification and of wise moral teaching. Imagine our surprise when, on turning to page 9, devoted to the 6th and 9th commandments, we found, instead of religious and moral instruction, obscene expressions, lewd particulars, in fact a complete account of the most monstrous schemes of debauchery. . . . And it is in the name of religion that such productions are spread abroad!

Constitutionnel, 2 May 1825

The present followers of St. Vincent de Paul are perhaps not quite so divorced from worldly interests, and we feel that the zeal they show is not entirely altruistic. In these unfortunate times there is a taint of money in everything, and the missions, an institution wholly apostolic in origin, have not escaped entirely from this disadvantage. A circular from M. Lesurre, arch-deacon of Rouen, to the clergymen of his diocese, brings to our notice the existence of a society of the faithful of both sexes under the name of *The Propagation of the Faith*, founded in 1822 with the Prince de Croi as president. Now, this society is aimed at helping missionaries by prayers and above all by alms. Each member is obliged to donate one sou a week. . . . Every bishop in the kingdom is instructed to promote this association in his diocese. Finally, to give the right idea of its nature, it is sufficient to say that amongst the prayers prescribed there is one which runs: 'Saint Francis Xavier, pray for us.' Now we all know that this saint was a Jesuit.[3] We would like to believe, as we are told, that the proceeds of this new kind of tax are devoted exclusively to foreign missions, but it is impossible to believe that home

---

[2] i.e. bands of zealots who toured the provinces leading special campaigns to re-invigorate religion.

[3] By hinting that the missionaries were Jesuits the *Constitutionnel* could imply a) that their organisations were illegal in France and b) that they were working in secret to restore absolute monarchy.

missions have been neglected in the financial field. . . . We hear from Besाçon that the hiring of chairs in the town raised 11,000 francs, and the sale of crosses, medallions, scapulars, beads, flags, hymn books and books of instruction brought in 15 to 20,000 francs. Moreover, these are small items compared with the special gifts made by wealthy families. By contrast, trade has gone down and customs duties have declined considerably. . . .

Constitutionnel, 6 May 1825

The royal court at Nancy has shown the same wisdom and dignity as that at Amiens by refusing to take part in a procession of missionaries.[4] In general these sumptuous affairs, which compromise a religion that makes a duty of simplicity, begin to weary all men with reasonable religious views. These travelling shops peddled by men who preach against tradesmen whilst carrying on business themselves; these booklets at 2 sous a time, whose licentious expressions shock the modest reader and are as damaging in content as in language; these declamations that are more theatrical than Christian; and all this phantasmagoria aimed more at striking people's imaginations than at saving their souls, have given rise to serious reflection among honest folk. They repudiate in the name of religion all these fashionable excursions which hold more attractions for young clergymen than the peaceful and monotonous shelter of the presbytery, where virtues are practised without show and where the worthy minister of the gospel does not leave the altar of the God of Love except to help the poor and hungry and console the suffering on their bed of sorrow. The adventurous life of the missions is jollier, no doubt. The continual changes of scene; the sermons at dead of night; the whole towns roused and garrisons dominated; the young girls to whom one distributes and teaches hymns, odes and sonnets addressed to the divine muses; the sumptuous dinners, or at least dainty meals which consist of a succession of local dishes from all the regions visited; the senior officials of the government who come and assist at the launching of the mission and humbly take their orders for the day: here, certainly, is more enjoyment for a priest who likes to get about and who fears boredom than that offered by the simple and poverty-stricken life of a country parson, who lives all the year round on the fruits of his garden and the income provided by his small stipend and slender fees. . . .

Constitutionnel, 9 May 1825

[4] The *Constitutionnel* lost no opportunity of flattering the magistrates of the royal courts, and of reminding them that it was their forbears, the *parlementaires*, who expelled the Jesuits from France in 1764.

We hear from Fécamp that *Tartuffe*, which has the charm of novelty now-a-days, was performed in the town on the 15th of this month. The crowds were so large that many people were unable to get in, and our correspondent states that nothing like it has ever been seen in Fécamp before. Molière's masterpiece was heard in devout silence, broken only by enthusiastic applause for all the digs at deceit and hypocrisy. The same eagerness and enthusiasm were shown at Nantes on the 12th of this month when the same comedy was performed. The *Ami de la Charte* informs us that the most important passages were applauded wildly and that all the inferences were smartly seized upon.[5] The Bretons, famed as they are for bluntness of character, cannot put up with the Tartuffes of today. . . .

Constitutionnel, 20 May 1825

(b) *The judgement*

In August 1825 the editors of the *Constitutionnel* were indicted before the royal court of Paris under the 'law of tendency'. Villèle had given cognizance of offences under this law to the royal courts in the expectation that the magistrates would be more authoritarian than the juries in assize courts, but he had reckoned without the anti-Jesuit traditions of the magistrates. The *Constitutionnel* was acquitted in the following terms.

The Court,
Having regard to the indictment by the public prosecutor, dated 30 July 1824;
Having regard to the 34 articles from the newspaper entitled the *Constitutionnel* cited as criminous;
Having regard to the law of 17 March 1822 on the control of newspapers;
Considering that, although several of the articles cited contain expressions and phrases which are unsuitable and reprehensible when used on so serious a subject, the impression created by these articles taken as a whole is not of a nature to undermine the respect due to the state religion;
And considering that there can be no lack of such respect, nor abuse of liberty of the press, in discussing and combatting the introduction and establishment in the kingdom of any association not authorized by law,

---

[5] The *Ami de la Charte* was founded in 1819 as a rival to the official *Journal du Puy-de-Dôme*. For a while it was dependent on voluntary gifts, but its popularity soon brought sufficient financial security to withstand fines and suspensions. Its anti-clerical articles were frequently quoted by the *Constitutionnel*. It became openly anti-dynastic in 1829.

and in exposing actions which openly and notoriously offend both religion and morals, and the no less certain dangers and excesses of a doctrine which threatens at one and the same time the independence of the monarchy, the sovereignty of the king, and the liberties of the people guaranteed by the constitutional charter and by the declaration of the clergy of France in 1682 (a declaration always proclaimed and recognized as a law of the land)[6]

Declares that there are no grounds for pronouncing the suspension that has been asked for, but that the editors of the *Constitutionnel* are nevertheless advised to be more circumspect.

Dismissed without costs.

Moniteur, 4 December 1825

3 Montlosier

The judgement pronounced by the royal court in the case of the *Constitutionnel* seemed to confirm popular suspicions regarding a clerical conspiracy. In February 1826 the Comte de Montlosier[7] published a resounding denunciation of such a conspiracy, which he believed was being fermented by the Congregation, an ostensible religious association whose ranks included many illustrious ultra-royalists. His pamphlet sold 10,000 copies in three months. The stir created by it not only discredited Villèle's ministry but divided the ultra-royalist party, for many members of the party, like Montlosier himself, disliked the new religiosity of the times.

The mysterious force which, under the name of the Congregation, exists all around us today, appears to me to be as confused in its composition as it is in its aims, and as confused in its aims as it is in its origin. . . .

Under Bonaparte there grew up, without opposition from the police, certain religious gatherings whose object was to fortify their members in the faith. This fact alone made them analogous to the old-time 'congregations'. At the same time real Jesuits began to emerge, under the name of 'Fathers of the Faith', and the two institutions naturally found themselves in agreement. . . . In 1808 the Congrega-

---

[6] The dangerous doctrine referred to here was the ultramontanism favoured by a large section of the ultra-royalist party. The Declaration of the Clergy of 1682, enunciating the so-called Gallican Articles, was promulgated as a law of the land by Louis XIV, but not all lawyers under the Restoration agreed that it was still a law of the land, since Louis XIV had renounced it later in his reign and the Charter of 1814 promised freedom of religion.

[7] François Dominique de Reynaud, Comte de Montlosier (1755-1838), came of an ancient but poverty-stricken noble family of Clermont-Ferrand. He had been educated in a Jesuit school, where he greatly disliked the discipline.

tion was founded in the name of the Virgin, whose name it bore at the time of the League, and from that year, under a known Jesuit, it has had, like the League, its leaders, its officers, and its president.[8]

Favoured by the events of the First Restoration the Congregation developed rapidly. The 20th of March[9] did not weaken it, but on the contrary increased its zeal and above all gave it a political colouring. It was then that it formed connections, which have lasted ever since, with movements in the south and with all the little Vendées that have arisen. . . . You must bear in mind that throughout the period which followed the ordinance of the 5th of September[10] the government was being swept along in an anti-royalist direction and came nearer and nearer to revolution. Every day the danger became more imminent. In this extremity the greatest efforts were called for, and appeals went out in every direction, rousing people and gathering them together. In towns large and small, in the capital and at court, affiliations multiplied. A secret postal service was organized in all parts of France. The correspondence was so widely distributed that even in the most remote provinces the Congregation was informed of various matters which were often not known to the government and not sent to the *Moniteur* until eight days later. . . .

The new electoral law was a great victory.[11] The Congregation seized upon it. . . . This was the time when Villèle rose to power. The Congregation itself urged his appointment, but did not respect him for long. At the time when its own power was not yet established it regarded his appointment as a stroke of good fortune, but when its sway was assured it was no longer satisfied with the appointment. Taking advantage of several defeats in the Chambers, the Congregation ventured to demand a new minister. . . . I have reason to believe that negotiations were opened in an attempt to appease the Congregation. People got the idea that the government and the Congregation were going to be merged. Already the Post Office, the Paris police, and the general headquarters of police had been given to members of the Congregation: it remained only to enrol the leading ministers themselves.[12] I cannot

---

[8] The League was a militant Catholic organization of the sixteenth century, under whose cover a section of the French nobility led by the House of Guise had sought to obtain power.

[9] The date on which Napoleon re-entered the Tuileries in 1815 to rule for the Hundred Days.

[10] The decree of 5 September 1816 by which Louis XVIII dissolved the Chambre Introuvable.   [11] The law of the Double Vote.

[12] De Mézy, Director-general of Posts, was replaced by the Duc de Doudeauville. Two members of the Congregation, Franchey d'Esperey and Delavau, were appointed director and prefect of police respectively.

say, nor do I wish to say anything positive: I only know that the most ridiculous rumours on these lines were flying about.

The Congregation was not content with having taken over the Post Office and the two police departments and with having to some extent reduced the government to subjection: its dissemination throughout the kingdom gave rise to a new system of espionage. Spying was formerly a mercenary occupation confined to low types of person. Now it is demanded of men of honour. The tasks imposed by the Congregation suggest that it has become a matter of conscience. Soon it will be regarded as a title of nobility. In this respect the lower classes of society have been treated like the upper. By means of an association called after St. Joseph, all workers are today regimented and disciplined. There is in each district a type of centurion who is a citizen of importance in the arrondissement. The commander-in-chief is the abbé L, who is secretly a Jesuit. Through the influence of an important personage he has just had the Grand Commun at Versailles handed over to him. There he proposes to assemble eight to ten thousand workers from the provinces, in a general headquarters as it were. Enormous expense has already been incurred in putting this building into a fit state to house those enlisted. . . .[13]

At the same time as disciplining the workers, they have not forgotten the wine-sellers. Some of these have been appointed to supply their drinks cheap. Whilst a man is getting drunk he is given set forms of words to say or prayers to recite. They have even taken steps to gain control of finding jobs for servants. In Paris I have come across chamber maids and footmen who said they were approved by the Congregation. Country villages, court officials, royal guards have been unable to escape the Congregation. It is within my knowledge that a marshal of France, who had for a long time solicited a place as subprefect for his son, could only obtain it at last through a recommendation from his village priest to a leader of the Congregation.

I know nothing positive about the Chamber of Peers. As to the Chamber of Deputies, during last April people counted at one time 130, at another time 150 members of the Congregation. A deputy whom I was able to interrogate who is a member of the Congregation would

[13] The Association of St. Joseph was founded in 1822 by the abbé Lowenbrück and patronized by Lamennais. It aimed at providing workers with temporary accommodation until they could be placed with Christian employers. The Grand Commun, designed by Mansard, was erected between 1682 and 1687 on the site of the ancient village of Versailles. It contained kitchens, pantries and butteries and housed the 1,500 people who worked in them.

only admit to 105. People say that since then the number has increased ...

Montlosier, *Mémoire à consulter sur un système religieux et politique tendant à renverser la religion, la société et le trône* (Paris, 1826) pp. 17, 24-6, 28, 30-33.

4 The government position

In the budget debate of May 1826, the clauses concerning church finances led to an impassioned discussion of Montlosier's monograph in the Chamber of Deputies. In one of the finest speeches of the Restoration, lasting the greater part of two sittings, the Minister of Ecclesiastical Affairs tried to pour oil on troubled waters.

Frayssinous[14]: Gentlemen, since the opening of the session complaints have been lodged from time to time in this Chamber on the subject of the clergy. Observations have been made concerning their position within our new political system. Wishes have been expressed for the improvement of their condition and for their complete reorganization. These complaints, observations and wishes have not been confined within these walls; they have naturally been carried around the whole of France through the ordinary channels of the popular press. It is therefore, perhaps, not without importance for the tranquillity of the clergy that these matters should be discussed in some detail, that they should be seen in their proper light and reduced to their correct proportions. ...

The criticisms that people see fit to make of the clergy boil down to two. First, they are accused of possessing a fierce determination to dominate, which causes them to encroach everywhere and, as the saying goes, to subordinate the temporal power to the spiritual. Secondly, they are accused of a belief in ultramontanism and of a strong liking for opinions which are foreign to, and irreconcilable with, the liberties of the Gallican church. These two accusations I shall examine in turn. ...

At the heart of every Catholic nation there are two authorities – the one spiritual, established by God himself, to rule the things pertaining to religion; the other temporal (and whatever form it takes this too is part of the purpose and design of Providence for the preservation of

[14] Denis Luc Frayssinous (1765-1841), Bishop of Hermopolis, was created Grand Master of the University by Villèle in 1823 and Minister for Ecclesiastical Affairs and Public Instruction in 1824.

human society), established in order to rule in matters civil and political. . . . If there existed only one power, the spiritual dominating the
temporal, it would be true to say that we lived under a species of
theocracy. If there existed amongst us only one power, the temporal
dominating the spiritual, France would no longer be professing the
Catholic religion, though this is the religion of 30 million Frenchmen. . . .

But perhaps this desire on the part of the clergy to dominate and
encroach is to be found in some secret influence, in some mysterious
and mystic club or other, in some kind of occult government which one
cannot see but which is nevertheless everywhere; in other words,
gentlemen, for we must call a spade a spade, in the Congregation. . . .

Let us look at the origin and history of this formidable Congregation. After the fall of the Directory a great soldier rose to the head of
affairs. Under his firmer and more capable hands France breathed again,
and hope for religion revived. At this time, however, many churches in
Paris were closed to Catholic worship. Young men arriving in Paris
were for the most part deprived of the saving help of religion. Then a
priest, venerable both in years and experience, conceived and carried
out the idea of gathering together some of those arriving from the
provinces, in order to keep them in the religious opinions derived from
home or to implant religious opinions in them if they were unfortunate enough not to have any. I saw this association in its infancy. This
saintly priest received them at his own house, in a very modest chapel;
there he celebrated the holy sacraments in their midst, followed by
teaching appropriate to their age, their needs, their present situation and
their future destination in the world. There were no pledges, no
promises, no oaths, no politics, no bonds other than those of true
brotherly love, which worked for the edification and well-being of all.
It was, in other words, a purely religious association, completely free
and voluntary. . . .

It was perfectly natural that young men who knew each other well
and saw each other often should end by respecting and liking each other,
and that as a result they should try to be of service to each other.
Besides, gentlemen, amongst these young men who professed and practised religion there were some whose deep piety was combined with
real talent. I have known several of this type. Is it surprising that since
then they should have achieved high positions, especially in a society
where careers are open to all Frenchmen? It is true that capability is the
chief qualification for any employment; but it is also true that godliness
is no disqualification. The Apostle has said, not that it is sufficient, but

that it is useful in all things. Montesquieu, who cannot be suspected of an excess of devotion, has said that religion of some sort, even if false, is still the best possible guarantee of a man's honesty.

It may be that there are a few schemers mingled with the ranks of this Congregation: I just don't know. It may be, too, that some have put on a mask of godliness: I have not met any such, but one is aware that at all times and in all places men have been known to abuse even the most sacred things. On the other hand I have known many of these young men who were the pride and joy of their families and who, thanks to the Congregation, were able to keep themselves free from false doctrine and from every fault of behaviour in the midst of the corruption of the capital.

People imagine, would you believe it, that there exists a Congregation which is like a sort of web stretched over the whole of France, penetrating and predominating everywhere, distributing all the jobs, besieging the holders of power and the councillors of the crown, and in short presiding over our destinies. Gentlemen, I can understand that at this tribune one attacks the ministers and their conduct: this is a sort of public right of ours. But that one should accuse them vaguely of allowing themselves to be led (or misled) and ruled by some power which is unseen but which nevertheless knows the secret of getting at them – that is an accusation for which I must say, gentlemen, I see no foundation. Let me express myself quite bluntly. If any one of the king's ministers were to fall under the spell of this magic power it would probably be the one who, by his very functions, must be the least sheltered from it: i.e. the minister for ecclesiastical affairs and public instruction. Well, gentlemen, go back as I might over the acts of my administration; no matter how much I sound my conscience and question myself; I declare that I have never felt the yoke of this mysterious authority. . . .

And now let us turn to a development of a different kind which is causing a sensation throughout the kingdom. . . . I refer to the missions.

People seem to think that home missions are an entirely new thing. Yet if one goes back only two centuries one finds irrefutable evidence to the contrary. After the long and deadly civil wars which rent France upon the death of Francis I, it could easily be seen that havoc had been made of the faith and of public morals. Providence then raised up men powerful both in word and deed, who contributed effectively to the revival of the faith. . . . Gentlemen the same causes have produced the same effect with us. Amid our revolutionary tempests – amid that appalling outburst of godlessness and crime – evil doctrines penetrated everywhere, attacking and damaging the very principles of the moral life of the nation and planting germs of dissolution and death in the veins of the body social. How many were the churches bereft for a long time of pastors! In some provinces a fatal indifference held sway; in others savage godlessness. Extraordinary efforts were needed to fight this apathy and these frightful disorders. That was the origin of the new missions.

France has witnessed a large number of them since the Restoration, in the countryside and in the cities, including the richest and most thickly populated. Why, on account of a little misplaced zeal, a few indiscreet words, a few fleeting disturbances (often exaggerated) for which the missions have been the pretext, should we forget the immense good they have done? Restitutions effected, families reconciled, marriages consecrated by the church, terrible scandals patched up or wiped out, greater respect for the Lord's Day, more alms distributed, more charitable associations founded for the relief of the sick, of prisoners, of orphans and foundlings – these have been the worthwhile results everywhere.

In addition I must point out that no missionary has ever presented himself anywhere without having been invited and authorised by the diocesan bishop and the parish clergy. As the number of ordinary clergy increases and there are enough pastors, we shall see a proportionate reduction in these missions which some people find so frightening. . . .

[*Second day*]
I thought I ought to get up and finish the speech which I began yesterday and to discuss the second of the accusations levelled against the clergy – that of a spirit of ultramontanism. . . .

Gentlemen, I seem to hear a voice raised in the midst of this assembly which is saying to me: We know very well that you yourself are a supporter of the liberties of the Gallican church, and we know that these maxims are still dear to France's bishops and to the majority of members of the lower clergy. . . . But is there not an insurmountable obstacle in the way of propagating these sound doctrines? Have we not, in our midst, a sort of Society which wishes to gain control of public instruction and preside over all the educational establishments in France, in order to direct all the youth in its own way and inculcate into them principles contrary to our liberties? Have we not, in short, in the midst of us, what we call Jesuits? (Much laughter).

I do not intend to go into detail concerning this famous Society. A few moments and a few words would not be enough for that: I would need hours, and whole volumes. I shall confine myself to a few reflections on the part they are able to play in the education of young people today.

There are in France 38 royal colleges, more than 300 communal colleges, more than 800 private establishments, institutes or boarding schools, 80 seminaries, and at least 100 ecclesiastical preparatory schools or 'little seminaries'.[15] Well now, there is not a single royal college, not a single communal college, and not a single private school which is in the hands of these formidable men known by the name of Jesuit. All these establishments come under the sole authority of the University, and are more or less controlled by the royal council and the minister for public instruction. And how many seminaries are there in the hands of the Jesuits, for it is there above all that they could indoctrinate the young and lead them astray. How many out of 80? Not a single one.

Out of the 100 'little seminaries', however, there are 7, gentlemen. How did they get there? Through a papal bull? On their own initiative? No, they were summoned by the bishops! From whom did they receive their spiritual powers? From the bishops! And could the bishops revoke them? Yes! Are they completely under the authority of the diocesan? Yes! Can he tell them to go? Yes! This has already happened – in the diocese of Soissons, for instance. So, we can boil down the vast influence over education that people attribute to the Jesuits to this. They have neither more nor less than the 7 establishments which I have just mentioned, and these establishments are schools like our colleges. They teach the Humanities, Greek, Latin, the secular sciences. They have nothing at all to do with theology, and I am sure that the pupils leave them without knowing the difference between us and the ultramontanes. . . .[16]

Some bitter and angry things are said nowadays about the clergy, and anything that seems at all unfavourable to them is given great publicity. What is the result? It is that today, as in the past, priests are insulted and ill-treated. This is a beginning. Public hatred is drawn

[15] The royal colleges were the state boarding schools founded by Napoleon and known as 'lycées'. The communal colleges were secondary schools supported by the communes. The seminaries were theological colleges. The ecclesiastical preparatory schools were not primary schools as their name would imply but secondary schools which prepared boys for the theological colleges.

[16] Frayssinous did not mention a factor which some people regarded as the most sinister thing about the little seminaries as a whole, namely, that they had ceased to obey the rule requiring them to take only such boys as were destined for the priesthood. With the connivance of Frayssinous as Grand Master of the University, these church schools were becoming rivals to the state schools.

down upon them, and from there, gentlemen, it is but a short step to the gravest excesses. It is not that I want to indulge in sinister forebodings. I am merely saying that we ought to be on our guard against anything likely to weaken the respect of people for the priesthood, and that if we deprive the clergy of the consideration that they need, religion itself will suffer. For it is no more possible to have religion without priests than justice without magistrates.

Arch. parl., *Chambre des Députés*, 25, 26 May 1826

5 Ultramontanism

Whilst the government tried to defend itself against charges of ultramontanism, critics from the other side of the arena denounced its professed gallicanism as tantamount to indifference if not to atheism. The following extract is translated from an essay entitled *Religion considered in its relations with the political and civil order*, published by Lamennais in 1825.[17] The government prosecuted Lamennais in April 1826 but succeeded only in getting him fined a nominal sum for propagating false doctrines.

Democracy, among a great nation, would inevitably destroy Christianity, because a supreme and unchanging authority in the religious order is incompatible with an endlessly changing authority in the political order.... We have now reached, under different forms and names, the stage of pure democracy in the political order....

The Charter, it is true, declares that the Catholic religion is the State religion; but what do these words mean? How can one see in them anything more than the announcement of a simple fact – namely that the majority of Frenchmen profess the Catholic religion – when this same Charter also declares that the State grants equal protection to all forms of worship legally established in France? Is it not a fact that the ministers of the various denominations are appointed or at least approved by the State? Do they not receive salaries from the State? Are they not each year allowed funds for the upkeep and building of their churches? Do they not enjoy as many privileges as the Catholic clergy? Are they not, in fact, treated in some respects more favourably? Now it

[17] Félicité Robert de Lamennais (1782-1854), ordained priest in 1816, had already made a name for himself with his *Essai sur l'indifférence en matière de religion*, published in 1817. In this work too he had described the Gallicanism of Restoration governments as tantamount to indifference. In 1831 his fear of the worldliness of Louis-Philippe's governments led him to sponsor liberal-catholicism in his newspaper the *Avenir*.

is obvious that the State which grants equal protection to the most divergent religions has no religion. It is obvious that the State which pays ministers to teach contradictory doctrines has no faith. It is obvious that the State which has neither faith nor religion is atheistic. . . .

In England the established church possesses huge revenues. Its bishops are by right members of the House of Lords and nearly a third of all the cases tried within the three kingdoms come before its courts. In France the clergy receive a salary, but the church itself is not endowed. What the State gives today, it can take away tomorrow. The church has no place in the body politic; it is of less account than a 300 franc voter. Without recognized rights, and without means of defending them when they *are* recognized, its appointed lot is one of complete nullity. An object of fear and jealousy to a government which oppresses it more than it protects it, it is not even left free to run its own government. Bishops are hindered from communicating with their chief; their jurisdiction is impeded; they are isolated from one another to make it easier to control them; they are not allowed to gather together according to the ordinances of the church; they are humbled to such a degree that it would be difficult to imagine a more profound state of servitude.[18]

If we turn from the political order to the civil order, there again we find atheism. It presides over every stage of human existence. A child is born: it is registered just like animals are submitted to the toll on entering a town. There is nothing, in what the State prescribes, to call to mind the nature of this being made in the image of God; nothing to call to mind either the duties which await it, or its promised destiny. It could grow up without any word of Heaven spoken over its cradle: it could die without having known any religion other than self-worship, any ethic other than the criminal code, any divinity other than the executioner. . . .

What is religion to the government? What must Christianity be in its eyes? Sad to say, an institution fundamentally opposed to itself, to its principles and maxims. An enemy. And this applies whatever may be the personal sentiments of the men in power. The State has its doctrines, from which it each day draws conclusions in the form of legislative or administrative actions. Religion has doctrines which are diametrically opposed, and from which it, too, draws conclusions, in the teaching of conduct and faith and in the exercise of its pastoral ministry. There is therefore between it and the State a continual war, but one which

---

[18] The Charter of 1814 had maintained Napoleon's Concordat, including the Organic Articles.

cannot last for ever. It is inevitable either that the State should once more become Christian or that it abolish Christianity – a project as senseless as it is abominable, and one the mere attempting of which would bring about the complete and final dissolution of society.

F. de Lamennais, *Oeuvres complètes* (Paris, 1844) v, 118-43

V

ECONOMIC AFFAIRS AND SOCIAL THEORY

I Paternalism

The restored Bourbons were constantly regaled with pious platitudes assigning to them the rôle of father of the people. They appear to have thought that the rôle could be carried out by dispensing minor relief measures at times of special difficulty. The following announcements, translated from the *Moniteur*, typify their attitude.

The King has just sent to Lyon the Baron de Ville d'Avray, Master of the Royal Wardrobe,[1] to carry out an order for silk materials to be used in furnishing the royal palaces. Not content with this favour His Majesty has desired a sum of 8,000 francs, drawn from his privy purse, to be allotted to the poor and needy of the town. M. de Ville-d'Avray, when handing over this money to the mayor during a ceremony at the Town Hall, let it be known that the king's intention was that the distribution of cheap Rumford soup should be greatly increased.[2] The members of the welfare board have assured M. de Ville-d'Avray that they will do their utmost to ensure that His Majesty's wishes are faithfully carried out.

Moniteur, 3 March 1817

By an ordinance dated the 2nd of this month, the King has graciously granted to the Department of Gard the sum of 40,000 francs, to be used

---

[1] *Intendant du garde-meuble du Roi*. The nearest English equivalent was probably the Master of the Great Wardrobe.

[2] Sir Benjamin Thompson, Count Rumford (1753-1814) published in London in 1796 an essay in which he maintained that too much solid food was detrimental to health, and that great nutritive value was to be obtained from thin vegetable soup. Rumford soup commended itself to many continental monarchs as a cheap way of feeding the poor – Rumford himself had set up 'soup-houses' in Bavaria under the patronage of the Elector. In England the idea was killed by ridicule from Cobbett who described thin soup as all right for foreigners but an insult to Englishmen.

either for the relief of taxes or to provide compensation for the people
of the district of Sernach who lost their entire crops in 1816. His
Majesty by this act of kindness gives further proof of his continual
goodness and of his truly fatherly concern for his subjects.

Moniteur, 8 May 1817

His Majesty, whose fatherly solicitude extends to all his subjects, has
graciously taken into consideration the needs of the workers of the
town of Nîmes, employed in the manufacture of silk cloth. We are
authorized to make known to the public that an order for about 6,000
yards of flowered silk has been placed, and that to authorize the manufacture of this material the Master of the Royal Wardrobe is merely
awaiting the confirmation required from the chief manufacturers.

Moniteur, 8 May 1817

The prefect of the Rhône department, Lyon, 30 April 1817:
It is urgent that we bring to the attention of His Majesty's ministers the
unfortunate position of those sections of the needy which hide their
poverty from all eyes and confide the secret of their misfortunes to the
pawnbrokers', depositing there one by one the garments which clothe
their children and the articles which they use in the house. Our good
king, who loves to hear about the needs of his subjects so that he may
alleviate them, has put at my disposal a sum of 24,000 francs for the
redemption of all pledges to the value of 5 francs or under, deposited
between 1 January 1816 and 22 April 1817. Any balance remaining
from this sum will be used to redeem work tools over and above the
sum of 5 francs, such as combs and shuttles, which deprive the worker
of his means of livelihood whilst they remain in pawn. Seeing this
touching proof of the king's goodness the needy classes will find one
more reason for placing their confidence in his tender regard for his
subjects, and the rich for continuing to contribute to those charities
which they dispense with such zeal and benevolence and to which it is
our duty and pleasure to give due recognition. Everyone will hasten to
bless the name of a sovereign who marks each day with kindness.

Moniteur, 8 May 1817

2   Food supplies

During the ancien régime a tradition had grown up that corn should be sold
only at controlled prices and that local customers should be satisfied before corn
was allowed to leave the area. Restoration governments were beset with

demands for a similar policy. They alternated between maintaining controls for
the sake of law and order and experimenting with free trade for the sake of encouraging agriculture.

Minister of the Interior: Report to the King, 24 December 1817

Sire,

Your Majesty has desired me to submit a general report on the
administration of food supplies in France during the years 1816 and
1817. The extraordinary expenditure that Your Majesty authorized for
this purpose relates to the harvests of 1815 and 1816, and would seem to
be sufficiently explained by recalling those occasions.

In 1815 events demanded some far-seeing measures, the chief being
the suspension of exports which the previous year's glut had occasioned
as necessary to encourage agriculture. In 1816 the harvest at first
promised to be plentiful, but all the hopes that we entertained were
successively dashed, and great sacrifices became inevitable. . . .

The invasion of 1815 brought European armies into France. They
were spread out, at the very time of the harvest, over the regions which
produce the most grain. The north, the east, and even the provinces of
the west were occupied, and everywhere these armies consumed
enormous quantities of food, adding to the wastage which is an inevitable consequence of such circumstances. It was calculated that the
results of the harvest would be insufficient to cover the annual consumption, but there was a surplus remaining over from 1814 which had
not been used for export, and from this it seemed reasonable to believe
that a few precautionary measures were all that was necessary to conserve supplies and hold out to the next year without any undue worry
or difficulty. By an ordinance of 3 August 1815 Your Majesty confirmed the ban already placed on the export of grain and extended this
ban to all land and sea frontiers. Shortly afterwards you found it
expedient to refer to a special commission the task of framing and proposing such measures as seemed desirable to ensure the free circulation
of grain. The commission was also expected to indicate what measures
would be most suitable for relieving those departments where prices
rose too rapidly because of the failure of trade, and even to make purchases, as need arose, in preparation for giving assistance with food-
stuffs at points where it would seem necessary.

Accordingly the Commission for Food Supplies was instituted by
ordinance dated 6 September 1815, under the presidency of the minister
of the interior. It set to work with the double purpose of assuring a

reserve stock for Paris and of giving assistance in kind to those districts where grain was or might become too dear. As a result, and in accordance with orders from the commission during the month of October 1815, 168,366 bushels of corn were purchased in the departments of Indre-et-Loire, Vienne, Maine-et-Loire and the Vendée, and were despatched to Corbeil via the Loire and the Orleans canal. Fear of causing a rise in prices in the departments where this first operation was carried out impelled the commission to complete the stocks required for the reserve with corn imported from abroad. A merchant received instructions to buy 2,101 tons of corn in Holland. These purchases were dearer than the first, either because of the cost of transport or because prices were higher abroad than on the French market. . . .

The departments bordering on Provence are one of the sources of supply for the town of Bordeaux, and the purchases that were made there influenced prices at Marseilles. This town, and also Rouen, normally look to the region around Paris to complete their stocks. The commission found itself forced to furnish some help to these three centres in order to prevent a rise in prices. During March 1816 a merchant was instructed to buy, partly in England and partly in the Netherlands, 98,750 bushels of corn, which were sent half to Marseilles and half to Bordeaux. A second purchase was made in April to supply the market at Rouen. . . . Finally, during June 1816, when the town of Bordeaux found itself entirely without grain, the commission was forced to make purchases in the departments of western France. . . .

At the beginning of the harvest of 1816, the earliest signs seemed most favourable. Then the rain came. At first it was confined to certain localities, but it soon spread generally, both in France and in Europe. Yet it was so irregular over the country that seldom has one seen such apparently well-founded fears succeeded so rapidly by hopes that seemed equally justified. The hay harvest was spoilt in all areas, and this early misfortune, which reduced the stocks normally used for feeding the animals, had an adverse effect on the consumption of grain. The rain which prevented the corn from ripening and caused it to deteriorate in quality was followed by several days of good weather, and farmers pinned their hopes entirely on the more important crops remaining to be got in. These hopes were nowhere fulfilled. Already some mountainous departments such as Lozère and Aveyron had lost the chance of harvesting various kinds of corn because they were buried under the September snows. . . .

As soon as the Commission for Food Supplies received confirmation of this disaster, and before the extent of it was known, orders were given for large quantities of corn to be bought in the home market and above all from abroad. Various merchants were instructed to buy in Holland, Italy, the United States, and at Odessa. At the same time negotiations were opened on the Barbary coast. . . .

On 15 October 1816 the average price of corn throughout the kingdom was 10 francs a bushel, making an increase of some 60 centimes between the average price in 1816 and the highest price reached during the previous fifteen years. This high price of corn was the cause of the unrest which spread amongst the people and of the disturbances which broke out at the beginning of the winter. During the first few days of November there was quite a serious insurrection at Toulouse; people refused to buy corn at the price fixed and tried to steal it from the markets. Order was only restored with difficulty, after the disturbance had gone on for several days. On 1 November the inhabitants of some of the communes in the canton of Vendôme (department of Loire-et-Cher) got together in gangs to stop the grain convoys, and the gendarmes who tried to disperse the mobs were repulsed. Troops had to be sent to protect the markets and the departure of wagons loaded with produce. In the departments of Loire-Inférieure and the Vendée people several times tried to stop the loading of grain into boats for transit elsewhere. The departments of Vienne and Haute Vienne were equally disturbed. About the middle of November there was a rising at Chatellerault which looked like becoming serious. In the department of Cher, although this was an area which produced plenty of corn, the canton and town of Vierzon were continually rioting against its removal. The arrondissements of Yvetot and Dieppe, some markets at Le Havre and Neufchâtel (Seine-Inférieure), and some in the department of Eure were the scene of trouble and pillaging. Peasants and unemployed workers roamed about the countryside stealing grain or demanding money from isolated farmhouses. It was necessary to organize patrols along the main roads to put down these disorders and protect navigation along the Seine.

As Your Majesty regretfully saw, any efforts the government might make were bound to fall short of that kind of a situation. With all its resources and every means of credit, it could do no more than maintain law and order and temper the extremes of misery. . . .

Signed, Laîné[3]

Moniteur, 7 February 181 8

---

[3] Étienne Henri Joachim, vicomte de Laîné (1767–1835), was appointed minister of the interior in Richelieu's right-centre government in May 1816. He resigned office in December 1881 when the rise of Decazes brought a slight swing to the left.

3   Control of the workers

To most governments in the early nineteenth century, workers were merely an aspect of law and order. French officials of the Restoration shared this attitude, but differed among themselves as to whether the workers could safely be ignored or whether it was advisable to carry out strictly the methods of control inherited from previous governments.

Police bulletin, Paris, 1 October 1817

The working class is composed of thousands of individuals, and the most industrious find fairly regular work in the various concerns, but the rejects form a vague mass of some hundreds of workers of all trades who, because of lack of employment, seek a living either in the casual jobs which result from individual enterprise or in those which arise out of the needs or the welfare measures of the government. . . . In observing the attitude of this type of person, one finds that they have no opinions beyond those which result from consciousness of their needs, and the only thing that concerns them is the certainty or uncertainty of their means of subsistence. Beyond this they are more or less resigned to their discomforts. The time is gone when one need fear that they will take to crime. They scarcely even talk of it, and if talk should go beyond the sort of back-chat left over from the Revolution and army life anyone indulging in it is looked upon as a police agent. The populace has learnt the meaning of fear, and there is more reserve on the streets than in the fashionable drawing rooms.

Arch. nat., F⁷3837

The prefect of police to the minister of police, 27 December 1817

In view of the disadvantages arising from the non-enforcement of laws and regulations relating to the workers, I have decided to remind mayors of rural communes and police officers in Paris of the provisions both of the law of 22 germinal of the year XI concerning factories and workshops and of the government decree of frimaire of the year XII.[4]

Article 6, section II, of the said law states: 'Any association between employers of labour, aimed at enforcing unjustly and improperly a lowering of wages and followed by an attempt to carry it out, shall be punished with a fine of not less than 100 francs and not exceeding 3,000 francs, and, if desirable, by a term of imprisonment not exceeding one month.' Article 7 states: 'Any coalition on the part of workers to

---

[4] 22 germinal an XI=11 April 1804. Frimaire an XII=21 Nov.-20 Dec., 1804.

strike, to forbid work in certain shops, to prevent people from turning up or from working before or after certain hours, and in general to suspend, impede, or increase the cost of labour shall be punished, if attempted or carried out, by a term of imprisonment not exceeding three months.' According to the terms of article 12, 'it is forbidden, under pain of damages, to engage a workman who cannot produce a record card[5] carrying a certificate, issued by the employer he has left, releasing him from his previous employment.'

Article 1, section I, of the governmental decree aforesaid requires that 'all workmen engaged as mates or apprentices must be provided with a record card.' According to article 2 this card must be endorsed 'in Paris by a police officer and in other towns by the mayor or by one of his deputies'. Article 3 is worded as follows: 'Independently of the execution of the law concerning passports, the workman shall be responsible for getting his discharge endorsed by the mayor or his deputy and for stating the place where he proposes to work. Any workman found travelling without a record card thus endorsed shall be considered a vagrant and charged accordingly.'

The provisions of the law and decree in question are primarily concerned with commerce, but they also assist in the maintenance of good order among the different classes of worker. I have advised that the greatest attention be paid to their enforcement, both in Paris and in the communes which come under the jurisdiction of the prefect of police, but the object I have in mind will not be attained unless departmental and local authorities throughout the kingdom exercise the same care over enforcing the provisions rigorously. The result should have the advantage, among others, of driving away from the capital vast numbers of down-and-outs who, under the pretext of looking for work in Paris, arrive here begging their way from village to village or along the roads, and finally come to the prefecture of police demanding free passports in the hope of obtaining the relief granted to the needy by the law of 13 June 1790.

Arch. nat., F[7]9786

4   Machine breaking

In 1815 the use of machines in French industry was still the exception rather than the rule. During the Restoration the firms which introduced machines often found themselves attacked by angry workers. The rioters were less well

[5] *Livret.*

organized than the Luddites in Britain, however, and the authorities, who did not hesitate to employ troops, had little difficulty in arresting the ringleaders.

Report of the king's attorney, Vienne, 26 February 1819

We, king's attorney attached to the court of first instance at Vienne, department of Isère, on receiving urgent information that today, 26 February 1819, at 1.30 p.m., the new shearing machine belonging to Messrs Gentin and Odoard had arrived on the bank of the river Gers close to its appointed destination, and that a great crowd of workers had hurried to the spot shouting 'Away with the machine!', carbine shots being heard and every indication being given of an intention on the part of the gathering of workers to use force in plundering this piece of private property, went immediately to the spot: whereupon the sub-prefect, mayor and police superintendent joined us in authorizing the use of armed force. . . .

Arriving at the entrance to the workshop of Messrs Odoard and Gentin on the right bank of the river, we saw in the water, at a distance of about fifteen feet, a wagon without horses, the shafts in the air, loaded with four or five cases of which one was visibly broken, and at three or four paces distant in the water an instrument made of iron or other metal, of the same size as the case as to length; various groups of cavalry and gendarmes both on foot and on horseback posted at intervals on both banks of the river Gers and on the heights, guarding all approaches; the windows giving on to the river being partly shut.

M. Desprémenil, lieutenant colonel of dragoons commanding the post, stated that shortly before our arrival, when the armed force had not yet got to the scene to disperse the crowd on the right bank, several persons in short jackets whom he did not know but whom he presumed to be workers flung themselves into the water and rushed at the wagon, armed with wooden staves and with a sharp iron instrument called a cloth shearer; that they broke open the first case that came to hand and threw one of the instruments which it contained into the water; and that they would have gone on had not M. d'Augereauville, adjutant-major of the Gironde Dragoons, and M. de Verville, chief of the gendarmerie, followed by brigadiers, dragoons and gendarmes, come up and stopped them, putting the assailants to flight in spite of a shower of stones coming from windows on both sides of the Gers. . . .

Edlon Montal (Jean or Pierre) of Grenoble or Beaurepaire, who served his apprenticeship as a cloth shearer with Bomières Junior in Vienne and is now working on the new road, is the man who used the cloth shearer to smash open the cases. Pontet, known as Simon, a worker at Donat and Boussut's, was at the head of the workmen, carrying a club to smash the machine. Jacques Ruffe, shearer, working for his cousin Dufieux, was on the wagon breaking open the cases and throwing them into the water. The daughter of Claude Tonnerieux, butcher, threw stones at the dragoons and incited the workers with cries of 'Go on! Smash 'em! Break 'em!' The woman Lacroix, who has only one eye, shouted in the same manner. Pierre Dejean de Saint-Priest, working at Velay Pourret's, shearer, went from one workshop to another all day yesterday urging the shearing hands to gather at that spot. Bassett, weaver, is stated to have said, 'We shall do for the machine all right', and Rousset, of no fixed abode, made remarks such as 'We'll get Gentin' (one of the owners of the machine) and 'It's not the b—— machine that wants smashing.' [Other names followed.]

Being unable to obtain further information, we have asked M. Clement, superintendent of police, to hand in anything that may turn up later, and using our powers under article 40 of the Code of Criminal Procedure we have issued an order for arrest against the 19 persons mentioned above. . . .

Arch. nat. F⁷9786

5   Laissez-faire

(a) *A report on the operation of mule-jennies*

In economic affairs there was no sudden change in 1830. Some of the conditions and attitudes associated with the July Monarchy were present during the Restoration, though they were tempered by paternalism. The following report was submitted to the Council of Manufacturers on 25 April 1822.

Gentlemen: Some time ago you referred to your two joint committees on cotton and on hemp and flax two reports . . . pointing out an abuse in the manufacture of cotton which was detrimental to the health of young workers employed in operating the machine known as the mule-jenny.

The two reports, submitted by the prefect of the Somme, were drawn up respectively by the Trade Arbitration Council[6] at Amiens

---

[6] *Conseil des prud'hommes.* The *conseils* were jurisdictions existing within particular industries for the purpose of solving disputes between masters and men. Abolished in 1791, they were revived by Napoleon in 1806. Though elected by masters and men, a decree of 1809 which confined the franchise to persons paying the patents tax greatly weighted membership in favour of the masters.

and by a Health committee set up by the mayor of that town. They assert that to operate a mule-jenny by means of a crank, which makes a circle whose highest point is about five feet from the ground, it is essential that the person employed to turn it should be fairly tall; otherwise he is obliged to stand on tip-toe and thereby lose his driving force, or else to fling the crank round with a jerk to give it the impetus that he is not tall enough to give by following the circle round. The reporters for the two commissions make the observation that this action, carried out continually, is bound to be detrimental to the chest, which becomes weakened in a very short time and can, through inflammation, give rise to serious illness. Such danger is greatest when the person is young or not very strong.

The existence of this abuse is not due entirely to the selfish greed of manufacturers, however, On the contrary, the majority have made it their duty to prevent it. Often it is the parents, who, out of self-interest, are the first to give the children the fatal idea of taking up work beyond their strength in order to get higher wages. Moreover the dangers attached to this kind of manipulation are not confined to spinning: the carding, beatling and cropping of cotton present even more hazards to the health of the workers, and it should be noted also that crowding a large number of persons engaged in laborious work together in one place quickly causes pollution of the atmosphere, especially in cold weather when the doors and windows are closed to keep in the heat necessary for manufacture.

It is extremely difficult, not to say impossible, to take steps in this matter which are certain of achieving the desired aim. The government cannot prescribe such and such a process of manufacture. Persuasion is the only effective means, by Trade Arbitration Councils and local authorities, who must feel impelled by human kindness to visit workshops frequently to make sure that the desire for gain on the part of the owners or the workers themselves does not operate to the detriment of the health of the young people employed. . . .

The only appreciable improvement that one can hope for is an increase in the mechanisation of mule-jennies. The amount of waterpower that industry uses nowadays, and the number of steam engines installed, leads one to believe that very soon there will be few hand operated mule-jennies left; then the evils complained of will disappear of their own accord, or at least be reduced to proportions infinitely less distressing for mankind. Whilst awaiting this desirable era, one can urge the owners of spinning sheds to give particular attention to the work done by young people in their factories, and above all to use ventilators to purify and renew the air throughout the working day. It is true that this method will entail a little more expenditure on heating, but it should not for that reason be rejected, because it is a case of humanitarian action to conserve the health of the workers, whose feeble or sickly condition does far more damage to the interests of industrial concerns.

> G. and H. Bourgin, *Le Régime de l'industrie en France de 1814 à 1830: Recueil de textes* (3 vol., Paris, 1912-41) ii, 89-91

(b) *A report on the growth of mechanization*

The following report was submitted to the Consultative Committee for Arts and Manufacturers on 22 November 1823. It concerned the case of a man called Layrisse, of Oloron, who had invented a machine for finishing cloth, thereby causing unemployment in the town.

The question which presents itself here is a general question which can be answered without reference to the causes which have given rise to it. The substitution of machines for manual processes, if carried out too rapidly, can accidently harm the welfare of persons whose livelihood depends on this latter type of work. The crisis which results is a serious matter and a real disadvantage, but it is not quite right to call it an 'abuse'. The use of this expression leads us to believe that the prefect of the Basses-Pyrénées shares the opinion of those who believe that the introduction of machines will be prejudicial to the working class. The example of England, and particularly of Birmingham and Manchester where the population has increased tenfold since mechanization replaced manual labour, also the example of Lyon, of Louviers, Sedan, Castres and other manufacturing towns in France, is sufficient to dispel this fear once and for all. People forget that the substitution of machines for hands is never absolute: one will always need hands to work the machines and to build and maintain them. Moreover it must be remembered that ease and economy in methods of production tend necessarily to increase consumption, and what does it matter if one employs less labour to manufacture a piece of cloth if one manufactures a far greater number of pieces. Before the introduction of the stocking frame in France, stockings were knitted by hand, and whole provinces subsisted on this kind of work. Popular opinion rose against the use of frames: it was said that this invention would condemn thousands of unfortunate people to die of hunger. But what happened? Why, the knitters, who before this time went about barefoot, were in a position a few years later to wear stockings made on frames. . . .

In any case, there is no longer any point in asking whether the multiplication of machines should or should not be tolerated. They have become throughout Europe a necessity that one must put up with, or risk becoming inferior to one's neighbours.

As for the temporary reduction in labour which results from the introduction of machines in a given locality, the evil is real but it is not without remedy. Although the public interest is more important than that of any minority, society nevertheless owes some sort of compensation to those who suffer most from this state of affairs. That is the whole point of public charity: and who is more deserving of a share of its benefits than the poor labourer who asks nothing more than to work? We think it is the duty of the government to come to the aid of people who find themselves in this position, in the same way as for the victims of fire or flood etc. . . . Meanwhile we propose to authorise the prefect of the Basses-Pyrénées to take money out of the rates[7] with which to form a temporary relief fund for the workers who accidently find themselves without employment as a result of the arrangements made by M. Layrisse with the manufacturers of this town. This relief should be commuted into working hours as soon as possible. We are convinced that there, as everywhere, things will automatically return to normal with the aid of this temporary sacrifice.

G. and H. Bourgin, op. cit, ii, 209-11

6 Saint-Simon

The advance of industry, though embryonic under the Bourbons, already gave Saint-Simon a vision of a new society dominated by industry to the advantage of all. Claude Henry de Rouvroy, Comte de Saint-Simon (1760-1825) was a thinker far ahead of his generation. His plans for a technological and managerial revolution were little noticed during his lifetime, and it was not until the Second Empire that Napoleon III took them up in an effort to secure through economic progress the glory that had eluded him in other fields. Meanwhile the idea, thrown out here and there in Saint-Simon's prolific writings, that the state should intervene to secure labour for all men, was taken up by socialists during the July Monarchy, notably by Louis Blanc.

---

[7] *Centimes additionnels.* These were not 'rates' in the English sense, but a small addition which the local authority was allowed to make for its own use when levying the state's taxes.

It is an exaggeration to say that the French Revolution completed the ruin of the theological and feudal powers. It did not destroy them; it merely undermined people's confidence in the principles on which they were based, to such an extent that today these powers no longer have the force and credit to bind society together. In what ideas shall we find this organic bond which is so necessary? In industrial ideas. There and there only must we seek our salvation and the completion of the revolution.

Yes, sir; in my opinion the sole aim of all our thoughts and efforts must be the kind of organization that is most favourable to industry – industry understood in the widest sense, and including every kind of useful activity, theoretical as well as practical, intellectual as well as manual. By the kind of organization most favourable to industry, I mean a government in which the political power has no more activity or force than is necessary to prevent useful work from being hindered; a government in which everything is so arranged that the workers, who together form the real community, can exchange the products of their various labours amongst themselves directly and with complete freedom; a government in which the community, which alone knows what is good for it and what it wants and prefers, shall also be the sole judge of the worth and utility of labour.

> From 'Sixth letter to an American', *L'Industrie*, 1817 (*Oeuvres de Saint-Simon et d'Enfantin*, 47 vols., Paris 1865-78, xviii, 165)

Let us suppose that France suddenly lost her fifty leading physicists, her fifty leading chemists, physiologists, mathematicians, poets, painters, sculptors, musicians and writers, her fifty leading mechanical engineers, civil and military engineers, artillery experts, architects, doctors, surgeons, pharmacists, seamen and clockmakers, her fifty leading bankers, her two hundred leading farmers, her fifty leading ironmasters, arms manufacturers, tanners, dyers, miners, cloth makers, cotton manufacturers, silk makers, linen makers, and makers of hardware, china and pottery, crystal and glass, her fifty leading chandlers, carriers, printers, engravers, goldsmiths and other metal workers, her fifty leading masons, carpenters, joiners, farriers, locksmiths, cutlers, smelters, and a hundred other persons of various occupations, eminent in the sciences, fine arts and professions; making in all the three thousand leading scientists, artists and craftsmen in France. Since these men are France's most essential producers – those who give us the most important products, direct the concerns most useful to the nation, and achieve results in the arts and sciences, fine arts and professions – they are undoubtedly the flower of French society. They are of all Frenchmen the most useful to their country, contributing the most to its glory and advancing its civilization as well as its prosperity. The nation would become a lifeless body the moment that it lost them. . . . It would take France at least a generation to recover from this misfortune, for men who distinguish themselves in work of positive value are truly exceptional, and nature is not lavish with exceptions, especially of this kind.

Let us move on now to another assumption. Suppose that France preserved all the men of genius she possessed in the arts and sciences, fine arts and professions, but that instead she had the misfortune to lose in one day Monsieur the king's brother, Monseigneur the Duc d'Angoulême, Monseigneur the Duc de Berry, Monseigneur the Duc d'Orléans, Monseigneur the Duc de Bourbon, Madame the Duchesse d'Angoulême, Madame the Duchesse de Berry, Madame the Duchesse de Bourbon, and Mademoiselle de Condé. Suppose that France lost at the same time all the great officers of the royal household, all the ministers of state (with or without portfolio), all the councillors of state, all the chief magistrates, all the marshals, all the cardinals, archbishops, bishops, vicars general and canons, all the prefects and sub-prefects, all the employees in government offices, all the judges, and in addition the ten thousand richest landowners who live on the rents of their estates. This accident would certainly distress the French, because they are kind-hearted and could not see with indifference the sudden disappearance of so large a number of their countrymen; but the loss of these thirty thousand individuals, who are reputed to be the most important in the state, would not grieve them for a moment for anything but sentimental reasons, for they would be no great political loss to the state.

To start with, it would be very easy to fill the places that were left vacant. There are plenty of Frenchmen who could exercise the functions of the king's brother as well as Monsieur, plenty who are capable of occupying the position of prince just as well as Monseigneur the Duc d'Angoulême, Monseigneur the Duc de Berry, Monseigneur the Duc d'Orléans and Monseigneur the Duc de Bourbon, plenty of French-women who would be as good princesses as Madame the Duchesse d'Angoulême or Madame the Duchesse de Berry. . . . The antecham-bers of the palace are full of courtiers ready to fill the places of the great court officials; the army has heaps of soldiers who would be just as good leaders as our present marshals. How many junior officials would make ministers of state! How many civil servants would be better able to carry on the business of their departments than the present prefects and sub-prefects! . . . As for the ten thousand idle landowners, their heirs would need no apprenticeship to do the honours of their drawing rooms as well as they.

Prosperity cannot come about in France except through the progress of the arts and sciences, fine arts and professions. The princes, great court officials, bishops, marshals of France, prefects and idle landowners contribute nothing directly to the progress of the arts and sciences, fine arts and professions. Far from contributing to them they can only hinder them, since they strive to prolong the preponderence exercised to this day by hypothetical theories over scientific knowledge. They inevitably harm the prosperity of the nation by depriving, as they do, the scholars, artists and craftsmen of the high esteem to which they are entitled. They harm it because they expend their wealth in a way which is of no direct use to the arts and sciences, fine arts and professions. They harm it because they draw off annually, from the taxes paid by the nation, a sum of three or four hundred millions under the heading of appointments, pensions, gifts, compensation, etc., as payment for their useless activities. . . .

These suppositions show that present-day society is in fact upside down.[8]   From L'Organisateur, 1819 (Oeuvres, op. cit., xx, 17-24)

The mechanism of social organization was necessarily very complicated as long as the majority of individuals remained in such a state of ignorance and improvidence that they were incapable of administering their own affairs. In this incomplete state of intellectual development they were still a prey to brutal passions which impelled them towards insurrection and consequently towards every kind of disorder. In such a state of affairs, which necessarily preceded a better order of society, the minority was obliged to organise itself on military lines, with exclusive control over legislation, and to frame the law in such a manner as to keep all power to itself and hold the majority in tutelage. . . . Today this state of affairs can and should be completely altered. The main effort should be directed to the improvement of our moral and physical welfare, since only a small amount of force is now required to maintain public order. The majority have become used to work (which eliminates any tendency towards disorder) and now consists of men who have proved recently that they are capable of administering property, whether in land or money. . . .

The most direct method of improving the moral and physical con-

[8] Saint-Simon won a brief notoriety when he was prosecuted for contempt of the roya family in this article. He was tried in the assize court and acquitted.

dition of the majority of the population is to give priority to those parts of state expenditure which are necessary to procure work for all able-bodied men, to ensure their physical existence; also to those which are aimed at spreading as quickly as possible among the proletarian class a knowledge of positive science; and finally to those which ensure for the people composing this class the recreation and comfort necessary to develop their intelligence. We must add to this the measures necessary to ensure that the national wealth is administered by the men most fitted for the job, and most interested in doing it well, namely, the most important industrialists.

From *De l'organisation sociale*, 1825 (*Oeuvres, op. cit.*, xxxix, 125-8)

7 Fourier

The condition of the people was not yet the popular question it became under the July Monarchy. Among the few men that concerned themselves with it, Charles Fourier (1772-1837) was enough of a crank to be thought insane. Among his voluminous writings he put forward again and again plans for forming an ideal community, called a phalanstery, in which families would live and work together under perfect conditions, each contributing such capital as he or she could afford, each doing the work for which he or she was fitted, and each drawing dividends over and above a guaranteed minimum. These plans were interspersed with denunciations of the existing status of women and recommendations of free love, which frightened the middle classes.

Associative labour, in order to exert so strong an attraction upon people, will have to differ at every point from the repulsive conditions which render work so odious to us in the existing state of affairs. For associative labour to become attractive it will have to fulfil the following seven conditions:

1. Every labourer must be a partner, rewarded by dividends and not by wages.
2. Everyone, man, woman or child, must be rewarded in proportion to three faculties – capital, labour and talent.
3. Working periods must be changed about eight times a day, since it is impossible to sustain enthusiasm for longer than an hour and a half to two hours in the performance of agricultural or manufacturing tasks.
4. The work must be carried out by teams of friends, united spontaneously, interested, and stimulated by active rivalries.

5. Workshops and grounds must be such as to attract the worker by their elegance and neatness.

6. Division of labour must be carried to the utmost degree, so that workers of both sexes and all ages can be allocated to the tasks most suitable for them.

7. In this distribution, every man, woman or child must have the right to work or join at any time in such branch of the work as they please to select, as long as they give proof of integrity and ability.

Finally, and most important, people in this new order must possess a guarantee of well-being, of a minimum sufficient for the present and the future, so that they may be free from all anxiety concerning themselves and their families.

> From *Théorie de l'Unité Universelle*, first pub-
> lished in Paris in 1822 (*Oeuvres complètes de
> Charles Fourier*, 6 vols, Paris 1841-5, iii, 15-16)

It is upon women that civilization weighs most heavily: it is for women to attack it. What sort of an existence do they have nowadays? They live only by privation, even in industry where man has invaded everything down to the petty occupations of sewing and the pen, whilst women are seen toiling at heavy work in the fields. Is it not scandalous to see athletes of thirty years old bent over a desk or carrying cups of coffee in their brawny arms, as if there was any shortage of women and children to attend to these trifling duties of the office and the home?

What, then, are the means of subsistence for women without private fortune? The distaff, or their charms if they have any. Yes, prostitution, open or veiled, is really their only resource, and philosophy denies them even that. This is the abject fate to which they are condemned by that civilization, that conjugal slavery which they have not even dreamed of attacking. . . .

> From *Théorie des Quatre Mouvements*, first
> published in Lyon in 1808 and subsequently in
> Paris in 1841 (*Oeuvres, op. cit.*, i, 221-2)

The majority of marriages are often, at the end of a few months or perhaps even from the second day, nothing but sheer brutality – chance coupling provoked by the domestic tie, without any illusion of mind or heart. This is a very common result among the mass of the people, where the husband and wife, bored, surly and quarrelling with each other during the day, are forcibly reconciled at bed-time because they haven't the money to buy two beds; and physical contact, the brute spur of the senses, triumphs for a moment over conjugal satiety. If that is love, it is of the most mundane and trivial kind.

Yet that is the trap on which philosophers meditate in order to transform the most gracious of the passions into a source of political dupery, to excite the rapid growth of population and to stimulate the poor to work harder by the sight of their progeny in rags. What a noble rôle to give to love, in exchange for the freedom stolen from it! Among civilized people, love is made into a provider of food for cannon: among barbarians, into a persecutor of the feebler half of the human race. Those are the honourable functions which our so-called lovers of liberty assign to love, under the names of harem and marriage. Blinded by the vices of their policy with regard to love, they repel any suggestions concerning the propriety of free love. Ignorant and false concerning the proper uses of liberty, they want unlimited liberty in commerce, whose crimes and swindles cry out on all sides for the curb of the law, and they withhold all liberty from love, whose vast scope in the Passionate Series[9] would lead to every kind of virtue and every marvel of social policy. What a perverse science these theories of civilized liberty are: how completely opposite to every desire of nature and truth!

From *Théorie de l'Unité Universelle* (*Oeuvres, op. cit.*, v, 462-3)

[9] In Fourier's ideal community, the day was to be divided into phases or Series designed to satisfy the various natural instincts.

VI

THE CRISIS OF THE RESTORATION

1 The Polignac ministry

In December 1827 Villèle fell before a combined onslaught of liberals and dissident royalists. His successor Martignac offered legislative concessions to the liberals, but the latter would not be satisfied unless they were taken into office. Charles, however, was determined never to allow the Chamber to dictate his choice of ministers, and on 8 August 1829 he dismissed Martignac and appointed the rigidly aristocratic Polignac, for the sole reason that the latter promised to stand firm in defence of the king's prerogative. The *Journal des Débats*, organ of a parliamentary group of royalists led by Chateaubriand, came out with the following article, for which the editor Bertin was found guilty by the Correctional Tribunal of the Seine of attacking the king's constitutional right to appoint ministers. On appeal Bertin pleaded that he had not questioned the king's right, but only Charles X's use of it. He was acquitted.

So; the bond of love and confidence which united people and monarch is broken once more! We are faced yet again with the court with its old resentments, the émigrés with their prejudices, the priesthood with its hatred of liberty, coming between France and her king. What she has gained by forty years of toil and suffering is now to be taken away; what she has repelled with all her might and main is to be imposed on her by force.

What perfidious counsels can thus have misled Charles X in his wisdom, and thrust him at his age, when peace and quiet are essential to his well-being, into a new career of discord? And why? What have we done that our king should separate himself from us thus? Were people ever more submissive to the laws? Has royal authority anywhere encountered the slightest attack, or justice the least obstacle? Has not religion always been surrounded by respect? It is only a year ago, at this very time, that Charles X visited his northern provinces. We ask him to recall the tokens of love and esteem with which he was greeted. Those touching pictures of a father surrounded by his children became

a wonderful reality. Today he would still find faithful subjects where-
ever he went, but saddened everywhere by this unwarranted distrust.

What has constituted above all else the glory of this reign, what has
rallied round the throne the hearts of all Frenchmen, is the moderation
with which power has been exercised. Moderation? Today it has become impossible. Those who govern our affairs now couldn't be
moderate if they wanted to be. The hatred which their names arouse in
everybody is too deep to be forgotten.[1] Feared by the whole of France,
they will become fearsome. Perhaps in the early days they will mouth
the words freedom and the Charter, but their clumsiness in speaking
such words will betray them and we shall see that it is only the language
of fear and hypocrisy. Ye gods! What sort of liberty would theirs be!
What sort of equality would we get from them!

What will they do meanwhile? Will they turn to the bayonet for
support? Bayonets are intelligent these days; they understand and
respect the law. They cannot last for three weeks along with liberty of
the press: are they going to take it off us? They cannot do that without
violating the law passed by the three powers, in other words without
putting themselves outside the law of the land. Are they going to tear
up the Charter which gives eternal glory to Louis XVIII and power to
his successor? They should think again! The Charter now has an authority which would smash all attempts at despotism. The people pay
millions of pounds to the law: they would not pay two to the decrees of
a minister. Along with illegal taxes would be born a new Hampden to
break them. Hampden! Do we have to recall this name of trouble and
strife? O unhappy France! Unhappy king!

Journal des Débats, 10 August 1829

2   The ultra-royalist plan

Charles X rapidly became converted to the notion that if, faced as he was with
deadlock between a liberal Chamber and an ultra-royalist ministry, the constitution became unworkable, his right and duty as holder of sovereign power was
to alter the constitution. The idea was put forward most clearly by Charles
Cottu (1778-1849), a magistrate of the royal court of Paris, in a pamphlet published in March 1830.

---

[1] Jules de Polignac was the son of the Princesse de Polignac who had been Marie
Antoinette's friend. La Bourdonnaie, the new Minister of the Interior, was an émigré
remembered chiefly for leading the ultras in demands for vengeance in the Chambre
Introuvable. Bourmont, the new War Minister, had deserted Napoleon on the eve of
Waterloo.

Louis XVIII . . . ought to have realized that since, among the three bodies to which the Charter assigned legislative power, there was one which had to be directly elected by the nation and which had the special right of assenting to taxation, this body would of necessity exercise over the nation, and in consequence over the activities of the legislative power, a particular type of influence which neither the Chamber of Peers nor the monarchy itself could ever counterbalance. It was obvious that, whatever the character of the Chamber of Deputies might be, it would use all its constitutional power to force the king to choose his ministers from among the men who possessed the confidence of the Chamber. . . . Unfortunately neither Louis XVIII nor his advisers foresaw these *natural and legitimate* results of the Charter. And even today, when experience has demonstrated them in the most undeniable manner, royalists have the injustice to describe them as audacious attacks on the royal prerogative. This blindness on the part of royalists is one of the greatest misfortunes that could have befallen the monarchy, for not only does it lower them in the opinion of impartial observers, but also it renders them incapable of bringing any remedy to bear upon the real state of affairs. They are obstinately contesting the constitutional power of the Chamber of Deputies, in the teeth of the evidence, and wearing themselves out in vain efforts to prove to the nation that the Chamber's pretentions are illegal, when they should be thinking instead of a means of harmonizing it with the monarchy. . . .

In view of the inevitable consequences of the Charter, how ought the Chamber of Deputies to be organized? . . . Since the middle of last century the English constitution has been the object of general admiration in France. . . . Well then, do you wish to know how the seats in the House of Commons are distributed? All those people who parade the advantages of that House and strive so earnestly to introduce them into our Chamber of Deputies ought to learn that, out of 658 members comprising the House of Commons, 487 are nominated by individuals: namely, 298 by members of the House of Lords, 171 by rich landowners, and 18 by the crown, leaving, out of 658, only 171 which can be considered freely elected by the people – and even they are under the influence of the aristocracy. [Here followed an elaborate plan for altering the electoral system in France so as to eliminate bourgeois members from the Chamber of Deputies.]

Since the inevitable result of the (present) electoral system is to isolate the Chamber of Deputies completely from the Chamber of Peers and the Crown, by making the former the adjunct of pure democracy, there is bound to come some day a violent cleavage between the

Chamber of Deputies and the other two branches of the legislative power. When this cleavage takes place, what will happen? The Chamber of Deputies will demand that the king change his ministers and introduce such and such laws, otherwise it will refuse to pass the budget; and in doing so it will be acting completely within its rights. . . . The king, on the other hand, satisfied with the policy adopted by his ministry, will refuse to change it or to introduce the required legislation, and in doing so he too will be exerting his constitutional powers. Thereupon government will be unable to carry on, and the Charter will be brought to a standstill, *legally,* without any constitutional means of putting it in motion. At that point it will be necessary to resort to a means outside the Charter. . . .

And the question arises, where is that right? Where does that duty lie? Who can be said to have the power to reform the Charter? Is it the Chamber of Deputies, which is only an emanation from the Charter, or the king, from whom the Charter has emanated? Obviously as far as the monarchy is concerned the question boils down to the very simple one of knowing just the moment most favourable to itself at which to start this unavoidable battle. The monarchy cannot start too soon. Each moment that goes by adds to the difficulties that will be encountered. . . . The crown must dispose its forces silently – prepare its new electoral law, its proclamations, its temporary ordinances; then suddenly burst forth – declare the state in danger, and by virtue of article 14 of the Charter assume constituant power and restore harmony to all parts of the government.

Ch. Cottu, De la necessité d'une dictature (Paris, 1830) pp. 13-16, 19, 32, 36-7, 114-16, 117-19

3 The parliamentary confrontation

(a) *The king's speech*

At the opening of parliament on 2 March 1830, Charles X made a menacing speech which threw moderate men into the ranks of the opposition. The final sentences ran:

Gentlemen, . . . The greatest desire of my heart is to see France happy and respected, developing all the resources of her soil and industry, and peacefully enjoying the institutions whose benefits I have firmly resolved to consolidate. The Charter has placed the liberty of the people under the safeguard of my royal rights. These rights are sacred: my duty towards my people is to pass them on intact to my successors. Peers of France, deputies of the departments, I do not doubt that you will co-operate in carrying out the good that I wish to do. You will spurn the perfidious insinuations that the ill-disposed are trying to spread. If criminal manoeuvres create obstacles to my government that I do not wish to think of, I shall find strength to surmount them in my resolution to maintain law and order and in my just reliance upon the French people and the love they have always shown for their kings.

Moniteur, 3 March 1830

(b) *The Address of the 221*

The Chamber of Deputies elected a committee composed entirely of liberal members to frame its reply. The Address, as it was called, was accepted by a majority of 221 to 181 and was presented to the king by Royer-Collard in his capacity as President of the Chamber of Deputies.

Sire, . . . Hastening at your call from all parts of your kingdom, we bring you from all corners the hommage of a faithful people, touched once more by the sight of your all-surpassing kindness and revering you as the perfect model of the most affecting virtues. Sire, the people cherish and respect your authority. Fifteen years of peace and liberty that they owe to your august brother and yourself have deeply rooted in their hearts the gratitude which binds them to the royal family. Their reason, ripened by experience and by freedom of discussion, tells them that it is above all in matters of authority that ancient possession gives the most sacred title, and that it is for their happiness as well as for your glory that time has placed your throne above the fury of the storm. Their conviction joins with their duty in telling them that the sacred rights of the crown are the surest guarantee of their liberties, and the integrity of your prerogatives the necessary safeguard of their rights.

Nevertheless, Sire, amid the unanimous feeling of respect and affection with which your people surround you there has grown up a spirit of uneasiness which ruffles the security that France had begun to enjoy and taints the sources of her prosperity. If it is prolonged it could become fatal to her peace. Conscience, honour, and the fidelity that we have sworn to you and will keep for you always oblige us to reveal the cause to you.

Sire, the Charter that we owe to your august predecessor, and whose benefits Your Majesty has firmly resolved to consolidate, consecrates as a right the intervention of the people in the deliberation of public concerns. This intervention must be, and indeed is, indirect, wisely restrained, confined within well-defined limits; but it is positive in its result, for it brings about permanent agreement between the political views of your government and the wishes of your people, which is the indispensable condition of the orderly conduct of public affairs. Sire, our loyalty and devotion force us to tell you that this agreement does not exist. The fundamental attitude of the government today is an unwarranted mistrust of the feelings and opinions of France. Your people are distressed about it because it wrongs them, and anxious about it because it threatens their liberties. . . .

Between those who belittle a nation so calm and faithful, and us who come in perfect confidence to confide to you the sorrows of a people desirous of your esteem and trust, let Your Majesty in his great wisdom pronounce. Your royal prerogatives have placed in your hands the means of ensuring that constitutional harmony between the powers in the state which is the first and necessary condition of the strength of the throne and the greatness of France.

Moniteur, 19 March 1830

4 The coup d'état

a) *The July ordinances*

Charles dissolved parliament in the hope of getting a more amenable Chamber, but the elections resulted in the return of all but 19 of the 221 signatories of the Address, and a large majority for the opposition. On 25 July 1830 Charles X issued four ordinances which constituted a resumption of power into his own hands. The first three ran as follows. (The fourth convoked electoral colleges for September 1830.)

Upon the report of our council of ministers we have ordained and do hereby ordain that:
Article 1. Freedom of the press is suspended.

Article 2. No newspaper or periodical, whether appearing at regular or irregular intervals, whether already founded or about to be founded, and regardless of the contents, shall be allowed to appear, either in Paris or the provinces, without government authorization received separately by the editors and the printer. This authorisation must be renewed every three months. It can be withdrawn at any time. . . .

Article 4. Newspapers and periodicals published in contravention of article 2 shall be seized immediately. The presses and type used in printing them shall be placed under seal and impounded, or put out of action. . . .

In view of article 50 of the constitutional Charter; Being informed of the intrigues which have been practised in several parts of our kingdom to deceive and mislead electors during the recent operation of the electoral colleges; Having taken advice of our council; We have ordained and do hereby ordain that:
Article 1. The Chamber of Deputies is dissolved. . . .

Having resolved to prevent a recurrence of the intrigues which exercised a pernicious influence over the last operations of the electoral colleges; Intending in consequence to reform, in accordance with the principles of the constitutional Charter, the rules of election, whose drawbacks we have learnt by experience; We have realized the necessity of using the right which we have of providing for the security of the state and the repression of all criminal attacks upon the dignity of our crown by acts emanating from us; For these reasons, Having taken advice of our council, We have ordained and do hereby ordain that:
Article 2. The right to vote and the right to be elected shall be based exclusively on those taxes for which the voter or the candidate is inscribed personally, in his capacity as proprietor or tenant, on the registers of land tax, personal tax, and private property tax.[2]

Article 4. The Deputies shall be elected and the Chamber renewed in the manner and for the length of time specified by article 37 of the constitutional Charter. . . .
Given at our palace of St. Cloud on the 25th day of July 1830, in the sixth year of our reign.

Signed, Charles
Bulletin des lois, 8ᵉ série, tome douzième, 1830,
nos. 367-80

(b) *The call to resist*

On 26 July a gathering of opposition journalists took place in the offices of a new anti-dynastic journal the *National*, where 44 of them signed a manifesto in the following terms. The result was the overthrow of the Bourbon dynasty in the Three Glorious Days.

[2] The patents tax and the door and window tax were no longer to count as electoral qualifications.

It has often been said during the past six months that the laws would be violated and a *coup d'état* launched. People's common sense refused to believe it. Now, however, the *Moniteur* has published these memorable ordinances which are a most resounding violation of the laws. The rule of law is interrupted: that of force has begun.

In this situation, obedience ceases to be a duty. The citizens who are the first to be called on to obey are the journalists: they must be the first to set an example of resistance to the authority which has despoiled the character of the law. . . .

It is not for us to outline duties to the Chamber which has been illegally dissolved. But we can appeal to it in the name of France to stand by its manifest rights and do all it can to resist this violation of the law. . . .

The government has today lost the character of legality which commands obedience. As far as we are concerned we shall resist it: it is for France to decide how far her own resistance should go.

National, 27 July 1830

VII

ESTABLISHING THE JULY MONARCHY

1 The republican demand

Members of republican societies took the lead in the fighting against Charles X. After his capitulation they tried to dictate the terms on which the new régime should be founded. The following extract is translated from their leading newspaper, the *Tribune des Départements* (founded June 1829).

France is free!
She desires a constitution!
She grants to the Provisional Government no more than the right to consult her!
Until such time as she expresses her will through new elections, the following principles must be respected:
No more royalty!
Government entirely in the hands of the nation's elected representatives!
Executive power entrusted to a temporary President!
Participation of all citizens, either directly or indirectly, in the election of deputies!
Liberty of conscience! No more state religion!
Men of the army and navy ensured against arbitrary dismissal!
Formation of national guards in all parts of France! Defence of the constitution confided to them!
The principles for which we have just risked our lives we shall, if necessary, uphold by means of lawful insurrection.

Tribune, 31 July 1830

2   The liberal proclamation

The republicans were out-manoeuvred, however, by liberal politicians, who offered the throne on terms to the Duke of Orleans. The following proclamation was addressed to the French people by deputies at an emergency meeting in Paris on 31 July 1830.

Frenchmen, France is free. Absolutism raised its standard: the heroic people of Paris tore it down. Paris was attacked and her arms brought triumph to the sacred cause which had just triumphed in vain in the elections. A power which usurped our rights and disturbed our peace threatened both liberty and order: we have re-entered into possession of order and liberty. Let there be no more fear concerning the rights we have acquired, no more barriers between us and the rights we still lack!

A government which will secure these good things for us is now the prime need of the nation. Frenchmen, those of your deputies who are already in Paris have met,[1] and whilst awaiting the formal intervention of the Chambers they have invited a Frenchman who has never fought except on the side of France[2] – the Duke of Orleans – to act as lieutenant-general of the kingdom. This is, they believe, the quickest and surest way of bringing the policy of self-defence to a prompt and peaceful conclusion.

The Duke of Orleans is devoted to the cause of nation and constitution. . . . He will respect our rights because he owes his own to us. We ourselves will secure through legislation the guarantees necessary to render liberty strong and durable, viz.:

Re-instatement of the National Guard, with guardsmen taking part in the choice of officers[3];

Participation of citizens in the formation of departmental and municipal governments;

The jury system for press offences;

Responsibility of ministers and subordinate officials, on a legal basis;

The position of members of the armed forces guaranteed by law;

Re-election of deputies appointed to official posts.

[1] This refers to deputies who had been elected in July, only to find their Chamber dissolved by Charles's ordinances before it was ever convoked. The more determined liberals among them met in the Hôtel de Ville and drew up this proclamation. The republicans had been anxious to avoid giving any authority to these deputies because they were elected on the old restricted franchise.

[2] Louis-Philippe as a young man fought in the revolutionary army at Valmy and Jemappes.

[3] On 29 April 1827 a number of National Guardsmen in Paris (reckoned at 5 per cent of the total) demonstrated against Villèle during a review. Charles X retaliated by disbanding the entire company.

Finally, in co-operation with the head of the state we shall develop our institutions in the way that they should be developed.[4]

Frenchmen, the Duke of Orleans has already spoken, in terms befitting a free country: 'The Chambers are about to meet,' he informs you. 'They will look to the means of ensuring the rule of law and the maintenance of the nation's rights. The Charter will henceforward be a reality.'

Moniteur, 1 August 1830

3 The revised Charter

A few days later, the Chamber of Deputies effected its determination to maintain the political system established by the Charter of 1814, with a few minor modifications.

The Chamber of Deputies,[5] taking into consideration the imperative necessity which results from the events of July 26th, 27th, 28th, 29th and the days following, and from the general situation in which France is placed in consequence of the violation of the constitutional Charter; considering, furthermore, that as a result of this violation and of the heroic resistance of the citizens of Paris His Majesty King Charles X, His Royal Highness Prince Louis Antoine, Dauphin, and all the members of the elder branch of the royal house are even now leaving French territory; Declares that the throne is vacant, in fact and in law, and that it is indispensable to make provision for it.

Secondly that, in accordance with the will and in the interest of the French people, the preamble to the constitutional Charter is suppressed, as wounding the national dignity by appearing to *grant* to Frenchmen rights which belong to them essentially, and that the following articles of the said Charter must be abolished or modified in the manner indicated below. [The most important alterations were those which declared censorship illegal, modified article 14 to prevent the king from suspending or dispensing with laws, instituted general elections every five years, and lowered the age qualification for deputies to thirty years and for voters to twenty-five years. With these and a few minor amendments the old Charter was re-issued on 14 August 1830.]

---

[4] This list subsequently became known as 'the programme of the Hôtel de Ville', and there were many complaints during the reign of Louis-Philippe that it was never carried out.   [5] i.e. the liberal deputies who had been elected in July.

Thirdly, the Chamber of Deputies declares that the following objectives ought to be provided for in succession, by separate laws and as quickly as possible:

1. The application of the jury system to press offences and political offences.
2. The responsibility of ministers and other officials.
3. The re-election of deputies appointed to official posts with salaries.
4. Annual voting of the army quota.
5. Re-organization of the National Guard, with the men taking part in the choice of officers.
6. Provisions which give legal guarantee to the status of officers and of all ranks in the army and navy.
7. Departmental and municipal institutions based on an elective system.
8. Education for all, and freedom of education.
9. Abolition of the double vote, and the fixing of requirements for voters and candidates. . . .

Finally, on condition that these provisions and propositions are accepted the Chamber of Deputies declares that the universal and pressing interest of the French people calls to the throne His Royal Highness Prince Louis Philippe, Duke of Orleans and Lieutenant-General of the kingdom, and his descendants, in perpetuity, by order of primogeniture in the male line, to the perpetual exclusion of women and their descendants. In consequence His Royal Highness Prince Louis Philippe, Duke of Orleans and Lieutenant-General of the kingdom, shall be invited to accept and swear to the clauses and engagements enunciated above, and that he will observe the Charter and the modifications indicated; and after having done so before the assembled Chambers he shall be invited to take the title of King of the French.

Resolved at the palace of the Chamber of Deputies, 7 August 1830.

Moniteur, 8 August 1830

4   The republican reaction

The republicans, being a mere handful of the population, were obliged to put up with the arrangements made, but they did so with an ill grace. The following extract is translated from a newly-founded republican newspaper, the *Révolution*.

A few of the guarantees that we demanded have been inserted in the new social pact and accepted by the man called upon to govern us.

Those that have been refused – and we say this because we know we are in the right – will soon be written into it. Let us hope that they will not be written in letters of blood. . . .

A government has been organised; it appears to meet the wishes of the majority. We are loyal citizens; we shall not disturb the peace of our noble country with recriminations. But our very loyalty imposes upon us a line of conduct from which we shall never deviate. Avowed friends of the people – of working class people – we shall never cease to stand up for them. Truth alone will find a place in our columns, revealed in its naked beauty. Our daily recompense will come from satisfying our consciences, but our feast days will be those on which we see some of the links fall from the chain which still binds the majority of our fellow citizens to a veritable slavery.

We shall show that all the revolutions we have been through were made for the benefit of a single class, a privileged class, constituting a new aristocracy, which thrusts aside the other classes with all its strength. A profound study of history has long been recommended, but the recommendation has been ignored both by rulers and ruled. . . . The family which has just been hurled from the throne found no salutory warning in the history of the Stuarts; the privileged bourgeoisie, which at this moment is piecing together the sceptre that the people have broken, does not see that it is taking the place of that proud nobility against which our first revolution was chiefly directed. It does not see that . . . there will come a day when the workers will demand the rights that have been violated or ignored, and demand them imperatively if no-one has had the foresight to free them peacably. We have already indicated the methods for doing this, and it will be the daily task of our newspaper to enlarge upon them.

Révolution, 11 August 1830

5 The defeat of the democrats

An electoral law passed during the early months of 1831 merely lowered the financial qualification for voters from 300 to 200 francs in direct taxes. Democrats then fought to reduce the tax qualification for deputies to a minimum, but they failed in spite of the following speech by Lafayette. The qualification was merely reduced from 1,000 to 500 francs

Lafayette[6]: Gentlemen, whatever differences of opinion there may be

[6] Lafayette had first gained fame as a young man by going to America to fight for the colonies in their revolt against Britain. After playing a spectacular part in the early stages

regarding the electoral system most suited to the international position and intellectual ability of each nation, the one general truth that all the world must recognise is that the ideal state of political civilization is reached when every taxpayer can be summoned to take part directly in the election of representatives and is not hindered in any way in the choice of his delegates. For Europe this is still a dream, but it has been practised for more than 50 years in the United States. There, every taxpayer can vote, and these taxpayers include the militiaman – the National Guardsman – who has paid in the course of the year the personal contribution of one day's service. There, there is no question of a tax qualification for candidates, and everything goes off without a hitch. Such, gentlemen, is the power of popular education, of public spirit and of truly national institutions. . . .

If one cannot arrive at this stage of perfection, gentlemen, one must approach as near to it as possible, and when you have sought what seems to me an exorbitant guarantee in a tax qualification of 200 francs for voters I cannot understand why you should want another in the shape of a tax qualification for candidates. We are given the example of England, but the electoral system of that country is condemned by the vast majority of the people. Leading statesmen, who are now ministers, are proposing to change it. Besides, the old franchise in England, though badly distributed, gave votes to a far larger number of people with far less property than the bill on which we are voting. In the counties any landowner can vote, by virtue not of a tax payment but of a net income of about 50 francs. In some towns and cities there is an even wider franchise. . . .

I cannot understand this refusal to place confidence in popular measures and popular institutions. . . . The three greatest public evils that can afflict mankind are despotism, aristocracy and anarchy, and to combat these three plagues we must find our sources of energy and power within the nation itself; for after all we are all of us the French nation. Look at the National Guard, gentlemen.[7] . . . What has been the result of so democratic an institution as the whole nation in arms naming its own officers without control? Do you see among its commanders a large number of proletarians and agitators? I, on the contrary, see before me noble leaders and friends whom you could not accuse of the slightest political extremism. Is it not equally likely that if

of the French Revolution he revolted against its excesses but never lost his admiration for democracy.

[7] Lafayette was made commander of the National Guard during the Revolution of 1830, in memory of the rôle he had played in the same post in 1789.

some of the electoral colleges nominated a deputy who did not pay any taxes he would be a worthy man, of distinguished talents, rather than a reckless, trouble-making type who may have some influence in a riot but would have none in the Chamber of Deputies? Besides, you may recall that among the agitators who flourished during the most disastrous and criminal periods of the Revolution it would be possible to cite names of several men in public positions against whom wealth proved to be no guarantee.

Arch. parl., Chambre des Députés, 7 March 1831

VIII

THE POLICY OF RESISTANCE

1 Casimir Périer

By the beginning of 1831 the new monarchy was under attack from republicans and legitimists, in newspapers, secret societies, and in the streets. Commerce was stagnant and unemployment growing. In February 1831 a legitimist demonstration at the church of Saint-Germain l'Auxerrois provoked a savage outburst of anti-clericalism which spread as far as Lille and Dijon. On 11 March 1831 the king took as his chief minister a man who, whilst remaining strictly within the law, was determined to bring every sort of pressure to bear against dissidents.

Périer[1]: When the king did me the honour of calling upon me to form and preside over his council, I was of the opinion that this council should be constituted on the basis of principles stated and agreed upon by all its members. . . . The ministry was formed in an entirely constitutional manner. Its very responsibility constitutes its strength. All its proposals and all its measures will be the result of free discussion and general agreement. The day when this harmony ceases, the government will be dissolved.

The solidarity which unites us and which we have fully and unanimously accepted gives us the right to impose on our subordinate officials the unity that we have desired for ourselves. Agreement must reign in all parts of the administration. The government must be obeyed and served according to the spirit of its intentions. It expects unqualified support from all its agents. Without this support, authority loses its force and dignity.

The principles which we profess and from which we shall not allow any branch of the government to deviate are the principles of our Revolution itself. It is our duty to establish them clearly, without

---

[1] Casimir Pierre Périer (1777-1832) was a banker who had played a prominent part in left-wing politics during the Restoration. First elected to the Chamber in 1817, he was one of the few liberals who succeeded in getting re-elected in 1824. He signed the Address of the 221 but would not take part in the Revolution.

exaggerating them or watering them down. The principle behind the July Revolution, and consequently behind the government which derives from it, is not insurrection. The principle behind the July Revolution is resistance to aggression by the authorities. France was provoked; she was defied. She defended herself, and her victory was that of justice, unworthily outraged. Respect for vows sworn; respect for law – that is the principle behind the July Revolution; that is the principle behind the government which it founded.

For it founded a government: it did not inaugurate anarchy. It did not overturn the social order; it affected only the political order. It had for its aim the establishment of a government which was free but orderly.

Internally our duty is simple. We have no great constitutional experiments to make. Our institutions have been regulated by the Charter of 1830. Several important legislative questions have been resolved during the present parliamentary session: the next Chamber will pose and answer those that are left. From that Chamber, and from that alone, must we now await the final improvements that are being called for so impatiently. Until the day comes for it to meet, what can France require of her government? Action! It is essential that order be maintained, law be executed, and authority be respected. Society needs impartial order and authority, for without order and authority it is succumbing to a lack of confidence which is the sole source of our present difficulties and dangers. To tell the truth, the factions are weak; the trouble lies in men's minds. Uneasy and divided, they succumb to all sorts of fears and suspicions. Hence the rapid fluctuations between annoyance and discouragement on the part of some of the authorities; hence the falling off of productivity; hence, finally, the injury to private interests, threatening the prosperity of the country.... Our ambition is to re-establish confidence. We urge all good citizens not to give in; for the government, far from giving in, will not hesitate to put itself at their head. (Loud applause from the Centre.)

Arch. parl., Chambre des Députés, 18 March 1831

2 Resistance in the provinces

Casimir Périer died in the cholera epidemic in May 1832, but the policy of resistance, involving strenuous efforts to quell legitimists and republicans, was continued by the next government. The following extract, translated from the letters of Thomas, prefect at Marseilles, to Thiers, Minister of the Interior, illustrates the problem as it appeared to a provincial administrator.

Marseilles, 22 October 1832

My dear Thiers,

You have asked me to let you have my opinion on current affairs. Here it is.

The government is exposed to two factions which are equally set against it. It needs force to vanquish them. The chief difficulty seems to me to come from the systematic and hostile opposition which is making war on the government instead of supporting it. If the government had received frank and loyal co-operation in the Chamber of Deputies, the country would not have been afflicted by factions and the laws would have recovered their authority and the government its dignity. The sympathy and affinity between the parliamentary opposition and the leaders of revolt and disturbance outside is only too evident. The spirit of republicanism and disorganisation would disappear everywhere if it disappeared in the Chamber. Carlism itself derives its importance from this state of affairs. It would not withstand a government strong in the support of the nation's representatives.

It is no good digging up the past, but I am sure that the Chamber would have been better if Casimir Périer had cared to pay some attention to it. He believed that elections ought to be left to the good sense of the public, and in a large number of colleges it was found that they had been handed over without precaution to the spirit of faction. Far be it from me to advise the violent and fraudulent methods which were put into practice during the Restoration, but I do think that the government should use the influence which it has naturally at its disposal. . . .

Police control of the kingdom is very difficult these days. There are two factions to watch, both headstrong and equally hostile. The republicans have already received some sharp lessons, but I would not be surprised if they still attempted some sort of an armed rising. You must be warned in time and stamp it out. It is easier to keep a watch on them than it is on the Carlists. I have found as many agents as I wanted in their own ranks. I have used these agents to sow discord and suspicion among the extremists. They correspond with societies in Paris. They would go as far as armed revolt to copy an insurrectionary movement which had any success in the capital, but otherwise they will not undertake anything serious. . . .

Keeping a watch on the Carlists is very difficult. I have needed more agents and more money. That is how I learnt that their rising had been fixed for 28th April and then put off to the 30th because the *Carlo Alberto* was obliged to put in at Nice to re-fuel.[2] I was quite well organized. It was I who looked after this affair personally, for the central commissaire employed and paid by the commune is no use. I shall be writing to you frequently on this subject in an official capacity, because police control is becoming very complicated and more difficult every day.

Our Carlists are in touch with those in Paris. Before 30th April I used to see their correspondence, but the arrests made after that, and the con-demnation of Charbonnier la Guernerie in Paris[3] have caused the addresses to be changed and I have not seen any letters since. They are in touch with the Vendée, with Italy and with Catalonia. They always rely on foreigners. . . . You will not be surprised when I tell you that they have *agents provocateurs* among the republicans and are pushing them into disorder and anarchy. They believe this is the quickest way of bringing matters to a head. A republic would immediately bring foreign bayonets into France; moreover its excesses would very soon bring on a reaction, and the result would be a third restoration in favour of Henry V.

> J. Vidalenc, *Lettres de J. A. M. Thomas, préfet des Bouches-du-Rhône, à Adolphe Thiers, 1831-6* (Gap, 1953), pp. 20-23

3   Republican retaliation

One of the chief features of the policy of resistance was an attack upon legitimist and republican newspapers. By the end of 1834, 520 press cases had been heard in Paris, whilst in the provinces most opposition newspapers had undergone five or six prosecutions. The republicans retaliated by founding an association whose subscriptions could be used to pay fines and found new journals. The following manifesto illustrates the flamboyant language they usually employed.

[2] The *Carlo Alberto* carried the Duchesse de Berry from Italy to France, where she landed near Marseilles on 29 April 1832. On 30 April she called upon the Midi to rise for Henri V, the son to whom she had given birth shortly after his father's murder in 1820; but the rising, such as it was, petered out in two days. The duchess escaped in disguise and made another abortive attempt in June to raise the Vendée. She was arrested in November. The government wondered what to do with her, but was saved from its embarrassment by discovering that she was shortly to give birth to a child by a Sicilian nobleman whom she had secretly married. This provided an excuse for escorting her back to Palermo.

[3] Charles Charbonnier de la Guesnerie (*sic*) (1784-1867) was a member of the House-hold Guard under the restored Bourbons. He kept in touch with a list of old royalists after 1830, though it is not known whether he was fomenting conspiracy or merely dispensing charity. In 1832 he was arrested, kept in prison for 9 months without trial, then condemned to 2 years' imprisonment.

When the press is exposed to continual and heinous persecution by a suspicious authority; when it is exposed every minute to numerous seizures, monstrous fines and preventive arrest of journalists; when the incompetence or the unfairness of the government and the division of parties opens up a frightening gulf under our feet; the moment has come for every man who feels in his bones the love of mankind and whose spirit is that of a good citizen to pause, to search his soul, and to set out for himself the rule of political conduct which is demanded by love of country and by this threat to our rights. . . .

The founders of the Association for the Liberty of the Press in the departments of Puy-de-Dôme, Cantal, Creuse, Corrèze and Haute-Loire, considering that today, out of 23 million French people, 22,850,000 are deprived by the electoral monopoly of full and genuine representation and that their rights and liberties are truly represented and defended by the press alone; considering that since the Revolution of July the government seems to have declared war to the death upon the press, by indictments from its attorneys-general, numerous seizures amounting to real persecution, arbitrary choice of juries, monstrous fines which are virtually confiscation, and preventive arrest of journalists, which is illegal; considering that an anti-national government would be more culpable if it delivered the press to the Holy Alliance than if it sacrificed a province, for by losing a province France would only lose a limb whereas by losing liberty of the press she would lose life itself;

Hereby decree:

That the Association founded in the above mentioned departments is aimed at guaranteeing the liberty of the press and at promoting patriotic and popular newspapers. . . .

Arch. nat. CC 613

4 The September Laws

On 28 July 1835 a megalomaniac called Joseph Fieschi made an appalling attempt on the king's life. In the shocked atmosphere which ensued, the government managed to pass a series of repressive measures known as the September Laws. These constituted the high water mark of 'resistance' and remained in operation for the rest of the reign. The most important was the following press law.

Article 1. Any provocation to the crimes defined in articles 86 and 87 of the Penal Code,[4] whether producing any effect or not, is an offence

---

[4] Attack on the person of the king or attempt to overthrow his government.

against the security of the state. . . . It shall be referred to the Chamber of Peers in accordance with article 28 of the Charter.

Article 2. Insult to the king, when it is aimed at arousing hatred or scorn of his person or of his constitutional authority, is an offence against the the security of the state. . . .

Article 4. Anyone who places on the king blame or responsibility for the actions of his government shall be punished with imprisonment for one month to a year and a fine of 500 to 5,000 francs.

Article 5. Any attack upon the principle or form of government established by the Charter of 1830 . . . is an attack on the security of the state if it is aimed at inciting to the destruction or changing of the government. . . .

Article 7. Penalties prescribed by the preceding article [imprisonment for 3 months to 5 years and a fine of 300 to 6,000 francs] shall be inflicted upon anyone who shall have adhered publicly to any other form of government, whether it be in attributing rights to the French throne to persons banished in perpetuity by the law of 10 April 1832[5] or to any other than Louis-Philippe and his descendants; whether it be in taking the title republican or any other incompatible with the Charter of 1830; or whether it be in expressing the wish, hope or threat of the destruction of constitutional monarchy or of the restoration of the fallen dynasty. . . .

Article 20. No design, engraving, lithograph, medal, stamp or emblem of any kind whatsoever shall be published, exhibited, or put up for sale without preliminary authorisation from the Minister of the Interior at Paris and from the prefects in the provinces. . . .

Article 21. It is forbidden to establish, either in Paris or in the provinces, any theatre or place of entertainment of any kind whatsoever without preliminary authorisation from the Minister of the Interior at Paris and from the prefects in the provinces. Authorisation is also required for the plays presented there. . . .

Bulletin des lois, 9ᵉ série, tome VII, 1836, No. 155

5   Fanaticism and despair

Opposition, other than in the mildest forms, was denied legitimate expression

[5] i.e. Charles X and his descendants, and the Bonaparte family.

by the September Laws. Respectable republicans confined themselves to criticisms of foreign policy and attacks on corruption. Fanatics tried to assassinate Louis-Philippe. One of the would-be assassins, Alibaud,[6] aroused considerable interest at his trial before the Chamber of Peers by refusing to deny that he had intended to kill the king and refusing to admit that he had had accomplices.

President of the Court: On the 25th of June last, at a quarter past six in the evening, just as the King, accompanied by the Queen and Her Royal Highness Princess Adelaide, was getting into the coach to drive to Neuilly, was it you, who, from a position in the courtyard of the Tuileries on the side nearest the gateway from the Pont Royal, fired upon the king almost at point-blank range a bullet which was later found inside the coach?

Accused: Yes, my lord.

President: Was not your object, in committing this horrible crime, to bring about an upheaval which would lead to the establishment of a republic?

Alibaud (in a loud clear voice): Yes, sir.

President: In other words, it was that which made you conceive the idea of an attempt on the king's life?

Alibaud: Yes, sir.

President: How long have you harboured this deadly plan?

Alibaud: Ever since Philippe I put Paris in a state of siege; ever since Philippe I wanted to rule instead of reign; ever since the king caused citizens to be massacred in the streets of Lyon and in the cloister of Saint-Mery.[7] His reign is a reign of blood; the reign of Philippe I is an infamous reign. I wanted to smite the king.

President: Take care, accused, or you will increase the seriousness of the crime of which you have declared yourself guilty – if it is possible to increase its seriousness. You will add to it a misdemeanour which is indictable and punishable in itself. When and why did you leave the armed forces?[8]

Alibaud: Two years ago, because I did not wish to serve the cause of Philippe I.

President: When you left the forces, did you go to Narbonne to the house of your parents?

[6] Alibaud was born at Nantes in 1808. After an elementary school education he worked as a clerk for a short time before joining the army. He deserted in 1830 because, he said, he did not wish to fire on the people, but he joined up again after the Revolution.

[7] Alibaud was referring to the fighting which took place in Paris at the funeral of the republican general Lamarque in June 1832.

[8] i.e. for the second time.

Reply: Yes, sir.

President: In 1834, your parents having left Narbonne and gone to live at Perpignan, did you follow them?

Reply: Yes, my lord.

Question: At Perpignan, were you not in communication with a certain number of refugees of different nationalities who were on their way to Spain?

Reply: I knew of one or two of these gentlemen who were on their way to Spain, and we arranged to meet in Barcelona.

President: With what motive did you arrange with each other to meet in Barcelona?

Reply: To overthrow the government of Queen Isabella, get rid of Don Carlos, and establish the republic in Spain.

President: Who was it who supplied the money for this journey?

Reply: My father.

President: Did you ask for or receive money from anyone else?

Reply: No sir, unless it was my mother.

President: What were your means of subsistence whilst you were in Spain?

Alibaud: I was only there a very short time. There were some people who had been lodging with my father and had not paid him, and they looked after me in Barcelona.

President: What did you do in that town?

Alibaud: I waited for the arrival of General Bigot, who was to put himself at the head of the Revolution. His following was to increase as he approached Madrid. Then Spain was to be revolutionized and the republic proclaimed.

President: Were not the exiles deeply engrossed with affairs in France at the same time as they were seeking to rouse Spain?

Reply: No, sir.

President: Did you not say, in the meetings you had together, that when a king became an embarrassment it was easy to rid the country of him? Did you not already manifest the intention of putting this doctrine into practice?

Alibaud: I don't think I said that; I have never said anything of the kind.

President: Was it not at least from the time when you left Barcelona that you were determined in your own mind to kill the king?

Alibaud: Yes, sir: at Barcelona even.

President: Why did you leave Barcelona and return to France?

Alibaud (raising his voice): To kill the king.

President: Were you not in contact at Perpignan, either before or after leaving for Spain, with groups of men who were actively engaged in armed conspiracy, either in the town or in the country?

Alibaud: I was never a member of any political society.

President: . . . What day did you arrive in Paris?

Alibaud: I can't tell you exactly. You could find out from the hotel where I stayed.

President: . . . How did you pass your time?

Reply: I followed the king about.

President: . . . What were you doing during the day of the 25th of June?

Alibaud: I left my room at half past nine and read the newspaper. I ate at ten. I left the hotel at eleven o'clock. I went alongside the Louvre. I saw the king arrive at mid-day. I went home and got my stick.[9] I went to a café and stayed there until four o'clock. From the café I returned to the Tuileries and . . . and . . . you know the rest.

Gazette des Tribunaux, 9 July 1836

[9] The murder weapon was disguised as a walking-stick.

IX

THE POLITICAL SYSTEM
AND ITS CRITICS

1 Governmental instability

(a) *Articles in the* Presse

The narrowness of the franchise under the law of 1831 produced parliaments in which most of the members thought alike on important issues. Parliamentary life consisted mainly of a scramble for places, not by parties based on principle but by small cliques motivated by ambition. Governments depended on shifting coalitions: there were 16 ministries in the first ten years of the reign. The following comments on this situation come from the first cheap national newspaper to appear in France, the *Presse*. Launched by Emile de Girardin in 1836 and selling at 40 francs a year instead of the usual 80, the *Presse* had 10,000 subscribers by the end of the decade. A fortnightly feature was the gossip column written by Girardin's wife under the pseudonym of Vicomte de Launay.

Behold, the politics of the week:[1] a round of tittle-tattle which the serious columns of a newspaper have no right to concern themselves with. The trickery, torment and trouble has been pitiful. Of course the general interest never counts for anything in these ministerial birth pangs. At the bottom of everything you always find rivalry – some petty but all-powerful rivalry that even women would not dare to admit to. A ministry composed of seven elderly coquettes (elderly coquettes being less easy to handle than young ones) could hardly be more difficult to harmonize than the ones we get. Mr So-and-so can't possibly stay in because of Mr So-and-so; this person won't come in because of that person; somebody else can't accept if another doesn't accept: it's a Chinese puzzle whose pieces won't fit. There are even two

[1] i.e. the last week in March 1837, when Molé's ministry formed in December 1836 was clearly disintegrating and numerous political combinations were being mooted.

or three which belong to another game altogether, and however hard one tries the picture can never be put together again. It is all very sad. Childish, no doubt, but fatal childishness; foolish, no doubt, but mortal foolishness. For every jolt weakens our strength; every tremor in the government shakes the whole country. Uncertainty, too, means death, idleness, discouragement, sterility. What plans can be made when one is waiting all the time? What enterprise can be undertaken when all is in doubt? How can one travel when the road is not mapped out, or sow seed on shifting soil? What would one think of a labourer who spent the whole working season wondering which of his horses to harness to the plough and had still not decided when the harvest came? That is the position we are in, nevertheless. Nothing can be done because we spend our days wondering who is going to do it; the whole convoy is stopped to watch the fighting amongst those who ought to be leading it; nothing is achieved; nothing moves except time, implacable time, precious time that we lose beyond recall.

Mme de Girardin in the Presse, 29 March 1837

For a person like me who is not very interested, for a person as detached, I might almost say as unconcerned as I am, there can be no more curious spectacle than the Chamber of Deputies. Men who individually are almost all capable, and who in a body seem quite paralysed; men who separately possess talent or experience or ability; men of true and undoubted worth who in private life have intelligence, courage, knowledge and wealth and who, gathered together in a political assembly at the Palais Bourbon, form nothing but a worried mass, without power, prestige or dignity. . . . Is it not a subject for endless meditation? Just see what noble elements go to compose the Chamber. There are brave generals to whom you would confide your armies, and you would do well. There are eloquent lawyers to whom you would confide all your lawsuits, and you would do well again. Yet all these united experiences, these joint capacities, these collective talents, these incorporated great men cannot succeed in the simple task of running the country's affairs. It is an inexplicable mystery. How does it come about? Perhaps it is because they don't bother.

Mme de Girardin in the Presse, 12 January 1839

(b)   *Lamartine's speech*

A ministerial crisis in January 1839, which finally pulled down Molé in favour of Thiers, provoked Lamartine into his most famous utterance, 'France is bored.'

The statement has been widely quoted as a judgement on Louis-Philippe's inglorious foreign policy, but the speech referred only incidentally to foreign affairs.

Lamartine:[2] The thing that strikes me is not what is lacking to the *Chamber* in the way of lawful authority,[3] but what is lacking to the prerogative of the crown, or rather to the normal working and free exercise of that prerogative. What is lacking, gentlemen, is majorities. Imagine yourselves in the king's position. Imagine you are sharing the painful vigils in which he no doubt searches with anxiety for the least signs and symptoms of a fixed and predominant purpose amongst you, so that he can make his choice accordingly and give his sanction to a cabinet which might have your sanction, and keep it if only for a few months. . . .

If you ask me why there is no majority, I say there is no majority here because there is none in the country – none among the electors. There is no majority here because there has been no great action and no great directing idea behind the government since its inception in 1830. 1830 was not able to create a course of action or find an idea. You could not re-make legitimacy: the ruins of the Restoration were under your feet. You could not go in for military glory: the Empire had gone, leaving you only a bronze column in a public square in Paris. The past was closed to you. You needed a new idea. . . .

You must not suppose, gentlemen, that because *we* are tired after the great upheavals which have shaken our country and century everybody else is tired too and fears the slightest movement. The generations which are growing up after us are not tired: they want to act and grow tired in their turn. What action have you given them? France as a nation is bored! And take care: the boredom of peoples leads easily to upheaval and ruin.

This 'idea' that I have spoken of I am not going to enlarge upon: it is a whole system in itself. I shall content myself with naming it. It is the idea of the masses – the idea of the organization and moralization of the people taken in its widest sense. This government was born of the people, so it should belong to them; it should be a government incorporating the interests of the greatest number. There, in my opinion,

---

[2] Alphonse de Lamartine (1790-1869), the famous romantic poet, was elected to the Chamber in 1833. He refused to join any political group, but became steadily more hostile to the government.

[3] The failure of the Chamber over many weeks to pull Molé down, when he was clearly discredited, caused many politicians to bewail its lack of power.

you have the mission of a new government in the nineteenth century.
(Lively support from the Left. Agitation.)

> *Arch. parl., Chambre des Députés,* 10 January
> 1839

2 Bribery and corruption

(a) *The government view*

In 1840 Louis Philippe at last found a stable ministry under François Guizot. The latter's success in retaining office for eight years was due at least in part to electoral management. The government made no secret of the fact that it expected civil servants to act as election agents. The following circular addressed by the Minister of the Interior to the prefects was published in the national Press.

Paris, 7 July 1846.

Dear Sir,

I send you the royal ordinance pronouncing the dissolution of the Chamber of Deputies. General elections are going to take place. This is another great trial for the destinies of our country. It is up to each man to do his duty in this decisive struggle. . . .

There is an extreme view which holds that the government should remain unconcerned and inactive and take no part in elections. These maxims have never been put into practice by any government. They are contrary to the very nature of our institutions. The actions, policy and intentions of the government are under ceaseless attack. Far be it from us to complain: it is a condition of representative government that all authorities should continually be under control. But what would become of an authority that was attacked relentlessly and never defended? The agents who are its direct representatives have a duty to see that its policies triumph; after all, they would not be serving it if they did not think its policies good. It is their duty to fight loyally and courageously against the machinations of parties, to put people right when they are being misled, to give honest people the courage of their convictions, and to assure the success of those principles of government which best correspond to the needs of our time and country.

What I am asking of you is that you exercise this frank and loyal influence: nothing more, nothing less. Freedom of conscience must be scrupulously respected: public interest and legal rights must never be sacrificed to electoral calculations. You must not seek votes for government candidates by seducing people with hopes of personal favours which they have not merited, or by threatening them that the exercise of their rights will affect the jobs they have lawfully acquired. Absolute obedience to the rules of justice during the course of operations, respect for liberty and morality at the polls, but strong and persistent action upon people's minds – those are the principles which must determine the relationship between civil servants and the public in matters of election. . . .

I am, yours faithfully,
T. Duchâtel[4]
Journal des Débats, 9 July 1846

(b) *An unsuccessful protest*

Critics believed that the government's practices amounted to corruption. Protests were occasionally made to the Chamber of Deputies, usually without success. The following protest signed by 9 electors did not succeed in unseating the deputy in question.

We, the undersigned, voters of the electoral college of Embrun and Briançon, wish to make, on behalf of ourselves and of several other voters who are not present, a formal protest against the election of M. Desclozeaux which took place on the 2nd inst. We declare:
1. That not only did the government and its agents fail to honour and respect freedom to vote according to conviction, but on the contrary it is known throughout the area that voters from the countryside were taken up and detained by their respective justices of the peace and kept under surveillance either by them or by other agents of the various government departments almost up to the time of the final voting; that employees of these departments took them out of public vehicles and led them willy-nilly before the magistrates, or into 'safe' houses, not letting them out until it was time to see the ministerial candidate and vote; that on the bishop's terrace in front of the court-house chosen for the electoral hall, voters were never able to talk or meet for discussion as many as five at a time without being scattered and dispersed at once by the gendarmerie, reinforced by neighbouring brigades and by the regular troops stationed in front of the college, each soldier with five cartridges in his pouch; that six voters who set out from Embrun on

---

[4] Charles Marie Tanneguy, Comte Duchâtel (1803-67) held various ministerial posts during the 1830s. He became Minister of the Interior in May 1839 and fell with Guizot in 1848.

Friday, 21 July, to go a little way to meet some of the electors of Briançon whom they knew, were immediately followed on horseback by all the gendarmes in the town. . . .

2. That these measures were so well arranged and agreed upon beforehand that a member of the magistrates bench who is a keen supporter of M. Desclozeaux said at Gap some days before the election, 'that if in 1842 the night of Saturday to Sunday had gone badly for the ministerial candidate at Embrun, steps had been taken this year to see that each doubtful voter was guarded by two safe voters and put to bed between them.'

3. That to persuade the voters of different localities to vote for the ministerial candidate it was made known that if M. Desclozeaux were elected great benefits would be obtained for the area. In accordance with these promises the inhabitants of Casset in the Monestier valley, who suffered from fire in October last, were given the sum of 9,000 francs. . . . At a dinner at the house of M. Baptiste, J.P., on 27 July last, at which M. Desclozeaux was present, the voters of the canton of Guillestre were promised the sum of 14,000 francs to rebuild the nave of the church. . . . A bigger sum still was promised to Romollon for its church. The voters of Rommollon, who number 22, were also promised that the road leading from their place to Embrun, via Rousset, which had been classed as a secondary road, would be declared a departmental highway and as such granted a sum of 25,000 francs. . . .

4. It is averred that some voters who support the government and the ministerial candidate have been on the list of voters for many years although they do not pay and have never paid the necessary quota of taxes. They include:

M. Puy, justice of the peace at Aiguilles, who only figures on the list in respect of properties which have never really belonged to him.

M. Davin, who has never owned and will never own the property at Embrun for which he is represented as paying the tax required by law, and who has been promised for a long time the position of J.P. at Tallard, probably in exchange for his vote.

M. Bleinc, of Argentière, who appears on the list by virtue of tax for property belonging to M. Bleinc his brother, who is parish priest at Saint-Bonnet.

The various agents of government departments, especially those dealing with indirect taxes, were put on the trail of voters. Influence was exercised over voters who hold official positions through promises of promotion or offers of better living accommodation, and over voters who do not themselves hold office by promises in respect of their sons, in laws, and relatives who are employed in government offices. . . . Briançon was promised an entire regiment for its garrison. A promise was also made regarding the revision of the Forest Code, which weighs very heavily on our mountain districts. . . .[5]

5. That, by an order of 28 July 1846, the royal court of Grenoble refused to increase the number of qualified voters to 150, in a college which has on its list:

    1 sub-prefect

   19 members of the magistrates bench

   19 inspectors, collectors or other finance officials

   19 public contractors or wine merchants under government in-influence

   14 mayors or deputy-mayors

In all, 72 over whom the government has a great pull. Hence placemen, added to those who mark their ballot papers,[6] form an immense majority.

Moreover, voters who were known to be doubtful, although they knew perfectly well how to read and write and included a retired major, were made to have their voting papers marked by pro-ministerial voters who were considered 'safer' than themselves. . . .

Signed . . .

Embrun, 4 August 1846

Moniteur, 25 August 1846

(c) *Statistical indictment*

In 1847, Prosper Duvergier de Hauranne (1798-1881), historian and parliamentarian of many years experience who had long championed the cause of electoral reform, published a startling indictment of the whole system. One of the most effective passages was the following:

According to the latest figures there are 61 colleges which have more than 800 voters, 139 which have between 800 and 500, 87 which have between 500 and 400, 95 which have between 400 and 300, and finally 77 which have fewer than 300. In other words, out of 459 colleges there are 258 with fewer than 500 voters, 172 with fewer than 400,

---

[5] National forests were rigorously policed according to a law of 6 January 1801. There were severe penalties for chopping down trees, and pasturing of sheep was forbidden. Rioting broke out against the foresters in a number of communes in the Jura mountains, the Alps and the Pyrenees during the Revolution of 1848.

[6] i.e. put some sign on them to show that they have voted for the government candidate.

and 77 which have between 150 and 300. To take only the last category, there are 77 colleges where elections inevitably depend on a very small number of families, always the same, and the majority of which, in addition to local interests, have personal interests to advance. Put among these families, for a few years, any authority whatsoever which is armed with all the forces of centralization and can bestow all the favours of administration, and tell me if the temptation will not be irresistible, almost always. Tell me if, as M. de Beaumont rightly remarked with regard to Embrun, the colleges in question are not all destined, inevitably and fatally, to become pocket boroughs of the government? It only takes a little skill, a little unscrupulousness, and a certain amount of effort.

There are numerous conclusions that could be drawn from these figures. For the moment I will confine myself to two observations. The two categories at either end of the scale are those colleges with less than 300 voters and those with more than 800. Of these two categories the former elects 77 deputies and the latter 61. In other words, if one adds up the number of voters belonging to the various colleges, 61 deputies represent 65,290 voters, while 77 deputies represent 18,047. Is this not a startling inequality which calls for immediate reform? If, further, one cares to work out the distribution of deputies of the government majority and deputies of the opposition as between the different categories, this is what results:

The present Chamber is composed of 459 members, amongst whom, counting double elections, the government majority can reckon 276 and opposition groups of all shades 183. Now, in the colleges which have less than 400 voters the government majority obtained 113 seats and the opposition 59; in the colleges with between 400 and 800 the government majority got 133 seats and the opposition 93; and in the colleges with more than 800 the government majority got 30 seats and the opposition 31. You will see how the government majority diminishes as the number of voters increases, until one reaches the real political colleges, where the opposition wins.

M. P. Duvergier de Hauranne, *De la réforme parlementaire et de la réforme électorale* (Paris, 1847), pp. 228, 310-11

(d) Guizot's attitude

Guizot stood out resolutely against every attempt to reform either parliament or the electoral system, however slight the measure proposed. The following speech, in reply to a proposal by Ducos and Ganneron to reduce the number of placemen and extend the franchise to persons eligible to sit on juries, typifies his attitude.

Look as I might, search as I might, I cannot find amongst us today, in the present state of society, any real motive for the electoral reform that is being proposed – any serious motive worthy of a free and sensible country. . . .

With us, the distribution of political rights is not and cannot be a subject for perpetual competition and struggle, as it is in societies which are differently constituted. The 300 franc elector perfectly represents the 200 franc elector or the 100 franc elector. He does not exclude him: he represents him, protects him, covers him, feels for him and defends his interests. Nor can the need to enter into political rights be felt strongly in our society. For however powerful human vanity may be, however natural the desire to exercise political rights, when this exercise is not necessary to the defence of daily interests, the protection of daily life and the safety of property, liberty and the daily well-being of mankind – when, I say, the possession of political rights is not necessary to these essential aims of society it does not awaken in the masses the same ardour. . . .

I say that the movement which has produced the proposal before us is a superficial, manufactured, dishonest movement, stirred up by the newspapers and committees. It has not risen spontaneously from the very heart of society, from its interests and requirements. . . . The primary impulsion towards electoral reform comes from the enemies of the government – from men who desire the overthrow of the established order. . . .

There are men who regard a large number of electors as indispensible to true representative government. In any electoral system they place most value on a large number of electors. To my mind these men are the timid and blind heirs of universal suffrage, which was the universal doctrine in France forty or fifty years ago. . . . I myself am the decided enemy of universal suffrage. I regard it as the ruin of democracy and liberty. . . . Not only have I no desire to see universal suffrage introduced among us, but I am opposed to every tendency in this direction. I believe it to be harmful and as dangerous to our liberties as to law and order. . . .

There is one further excuse, one final excuse for the electoral reform that is being suggested to you. It is described as insignificant. Even if it is unnecessary, even if it is not wanted by society, at least it holds no dangers, no real dangers. Gentlemen, it is, upon my word, a most

unusual argument to bring forward in favour of a reform, that it is
insignificant. I do not agree that it is insignificant. I do not agree that a
reform which is strongly solicited by the enemies of the established
order can be insignificant and hold no dangers. . . .

There remains one last point, on which I shall be very brief. Without
any doubt I am right in counting, among the motives behind electoral
reform, opposition to the cabinet and the wish to overthrow it. I am
not complaining of that: it is perfectly permissible. The only thing that
astonishes me is that it is not proclaimed outright. . . . No matter; I am
not arguing. I admit the lawfulness both of the aim and the method.
You are making use of your institutions: all right. I am going to tell
you what *we* shall do. As long as the majority of this Chamber does
not change the policy which brought this Cabinet to power and keeps
it there, the Cabinet will not let itself be overthrown by the minority.

Arch. parl., *Chambre des Députés*, 15 February
1842

3 Ridicule

Philipon's satirical journal the *Charivari*, which had been obliged to forgo outright republicanism since the passing of the September Laws, poked fun at the
electoral system.

There was a time when deputies represented the opinions of their
constituents. Nowadays they no longer represent anything but their
needs. . . .

There have been two distinct phases in this chapter of contemporary
history (a book which could only be illustrated by the caricaturist
Daumier). During the first phase, electors were content to demand of
their deputy, in exchange for their vote, some little service such as a
recommendation, a tobacconist's shop, a job as tax-collector, a cross of
the Legion of Honour or some other minor favour. Under this régime
the deputy could be described as a commissionaire. During the second
phase, when appetites had grown with eating, electors were no longer
content with this small price. In addition to services rendered to each
one personally, they demanded acts of munificence or beneficence to
the city. From being a commissionaire the deputy must become
Mycena. If we go on any longer the deputy will have to pave the streets
of the town with gold and light up the public squares with glittering
diamonds. From being a Mycena he will have to become Aboul
Kassen.

If today some naive candidate were to go to one of these practically minded colleges and say, 'Gentlemen, I ask for your votes because I am an honest man,' they would laugh at his artlessness and reply, 'What have you got to offer?'

– Gentlemen, my conscientious studies and the ability I have derived from them could be useful to my country.

– What will you give to the town?

– My vote will always go towards conquering the supremacy that France has lost, as well as to developing her liberties. National honour safe from all attack – peace firmly guaranteed – honesty in the exercise of power. Those are the things I support!

– Go on with you! M. Merluchon has promised us a fountain.

And they nominate M. Merluchon.

First we have Mr So-and-so, who was nominated because he established a pig market in the town; then Mr ——, who got a seat by improving a harbour; and now M. Charles Laffitte, who gets himself elected for Louviers by promising the town a branch railway.[7] M. Charles Laffitte arrives at the Chamber in a truck. His manifesto consisted of a sack of coal, and he ought to sit not on a bench but on a tender. These noble examples show amateurs the way in matters of election. There are constituencies where seats will soon have a fixed price, like goods in certain shops. Here, arrange for a barracks, and you will have a chance to conquer at the polls; there, build a theatre and you will enter right away upon the political scene. Gratify this city with a bridge, and the bridge will enable you to pass without difficulty from private into public life. With a clock tower you are sure of rising very highly in the opinion of the electors. Take care that your rival does not promise a higher tower. He may even cap you with a weather vane.

Before long we shall be seeing an auction sale take place at the poll in one of these honest constituencies, somewhat as follows:

– M. Berluquet promises a building to serve as a town hall. Any advance on a town hall? No advance? Going, going. . . .

– A town hall and a school!

– M. Dubuillon adds a school. Going, going. . .

– And public baths!

– Going, going . . .

---

[7] Charles Laffitte, a government supporter and nephew of the great banker, was declared elected at Louviers on 13 Jan. 1844. During the verification of powers it was alleged by the opposition that he was completely unknown in Louviers and had only succeeded in the election by means of promising a branch railway from Saint-Pierre to Louviers. The election was quashed. Re-elected three times, and expelled three times, Laffitte withdrew the offer of the railway: after which he was elected a fifth time and allowed to take his seat.

– A magistrates' court!
– Going, going . . .
– I will cover the monument in lead!
– I will sink an artesian well in the square!
– The last bid to M. Berluquet . . . Going, going . . . No further bids?
. . . M. Dubuillon? . . . Going, going, gone!

The price will be paid by the highest bidder, but it is public money which will stand the cost.

Charivari, 19 January 1844

X

THE DESIRE FOR GLORY

1 Republican dreams

In the early years of the reign, Louis-Philippe's governments were beset with radicals who insisted that France, having completed her own Revolution, should fulfil her revolutionary destiny by overturning the settlement of 1815, claiming her natural frontiers and going to the aid of other nations (Italians, Poles, Belgians) who were struggling to be free. The following speech, delivered in the Chamber of Deputies during a debate on Belgium, is a fair sample of radical oratory.

Mauguin:[1] Gentlemen, in the July Days France rose as one man and in a few short hours shattered the despotism of fifteen years. Obviously she must have been shaken by violent passions; obviously, bitter resentment burned in her breast. What was this resentment? I am not afraid to name it, for no-one will contradict me. She chafed under the yoke imposed by the foreigner; she remembered with shame the treaties of 1814; she shuddered at the name of Waterloo. Make no mistake – it was these ancient memories of glory and of humiliation unavenged that accounted for the success of the Three days. People were therefore bound to expect from the government called upon to direct the July movement some response to the sentiment that had aroused it. Something needed to be done to satisfy the will of the nation. What was wanted was for France to resume a position of strength and dignity among the Powers. That is what France wanted; that is what the July movement wanted.

You, Ministers, who have been the first to be called to direct the destiny of this glorious revolution, answer me! What have you done? How have you met this need for strength and dignity? Have you made the reparation for France's outraged military honour that she had a right to expect of you? Your first act of diplomacy has been to recognise the treaties of 1814 and 1815. I am not saying whether you did

[1] François Mauguin (1785-1854) had made his reputation as counsel for the defence in political trials during the Restoration.

right or wrong, but by that one action you gave the greatest possible offence to the nation. You recognized the spoliation of her territory. You took away even the frontiers she had in 1814; you ratified the abandonment of Landau and Sarrelouis and of the frontiers given France by Louis XIV. . . .

France, by the Revolution of July, broke her chains and avenged a great insult. She got rid of the agent and vassal of the Holy Alliance; she no longer wanted him. What has been the result of this movement that took place within the walls of Paris? All Europe has been shaken by it. It has made its voice heard from Paris to Madrid and from Paris to the Vistula. It has passed over Europe and created disturbance everywhere. The vibration is still being felt. You see how dangerous our example has been. Do you imagine that the sovereigns who are frightened by our contageous example will hesitate, once they have enchained their people and Poland has died defending her liberty, to come and quench the fire at its heart and threaten the walls of Paris? Ah! Keep your hopes! For my part I cannot share them. . . .

My reproaches fall on the principle of non-intervention. What is this principle? . . . The principle is that you do not meddle in the affairs of a neighbouring people; that you do not help the Belgians. So much I understand. Why, then, negotiate for such a long time in London?[2] If the Belgians are independent they have a right to choose their own sovereign. That is their first independent action. Why, then, exclude from this choice the scion of an ancient family for example? Why, I ask, exclude France herself?[3] France especially! Have you the right to renounce in the name of France provinces that have always been French? Of course I am wrong in saying that they have always been French, but ever since I was born Belgium has always been French to me.

Have you forgotten that a great man could demonstrate his greatness by refusing to sign this treaty which deprived us of our frontiers? Are you going to be like the Bourbons who came back and accepted a kingdom at the hands of the foreigners – whatever they cared to give them, as though it were something thrown at them? Is that a suitable response to the July movement and the need for liberty and glory which animated the French people?

Arch. parl., Chambre des Députés, 15 January 1831

[2] Talleyrand had been sent to London in Oct. 1830, to negotiate with the Great Powers concerning the future of Belgium, which had declared its independence from Holland.

[3] The Powers did not issue their Protocol until 21 January, but Mauguin seems already to have known that they had agreed that the new ruler of Belgium should not belong to the ruling house of any major state.

2   Bourgeois reality

Casimir Périer, in the speech inaugurating his policy of 'resistance', shattered all hopes of a radical foreign policy.

Périer: Foreign policy, gentlemen, is allied to internal policy. The evil and the remedy are the same for both. The evil, here too, is mistrust. People are wanting to make France mistrust Europe, and are trying to spread the belief that Europe mistrusts our Revolution. If it were so, gentlemen, Europe would be mistaken, and it would be up to France and her government to convince her of it.

Once again, let me point out that the Revolution has not instituted the reign of force. France is armed to defend her rights, but she knows how to respect the rights of others. Her policy is ruled by something other than passion. We want peace, which is so necessary to liberty. We would want war, and we would wage war, if the safety or honour of France were in peril, for then liberty too would be threatened; and we would call with patriotic confidence upon the courage of the nation. At the first signal France would be ready, and the king has not forgotten that it was in camp that he first learnt to serve his country.

Gentlemen, the principle of non-intervention has been propounded. We adopt it: that is to say, we maintain that foreign powers have no right to interfere by force of arms in the internal affairs of another nation. For our part we practice this principle, and we shall profess it on all occasions. Does this mean that we shall engage to carry arms wherever it is not respected? That, gentlemen, would be intervention of another kind. That would be to renew the pretensions of the Holy Alliance: it would be to succumb to the false ambition of all those who have wanted to subdue Europe to the yoke of a single idea and set up universal monarchy. Given such a meaning the principle of non-intervention would serve as a mask for the spirit of conquest.

We shall uphold the principle of non-intervention everywhere by means of negotiation. But the interest or dignity of France are the only things that will make us take up arms. We concede to no people the right of forcing us to fight for their cause: the blood of Frenchmen belongs to France alone. Never shall we fail to show a lively sympathy for the progress of European peoples, but their destiny is in their own hands, and liberty must always be national. . . . France will never exhort the world to liberty except by peaceful example. . . .

Arch. parl., Chambre des Députés, 18 March 1831

3 War fever, 1839-40

In the summer of 1839 Mehemet Ali, pasha of Egypt, made an armed bid against the Turks for the heredity pashalik of Syria. France, who regarded Mehemet Ali as a client, refused to join the other four Great Powers in bringing pressure to bear against him. Radical opinion in France howled for war on his behalf, as an act of defiance against Europe, and in February 1840 the Soult cabinet fell before the more bellicose Thiers. Palmerston, however, outwitted Thiers and isolated France by making a four-power agreement to curb Mehemet Ali. The war fever in France increased, but in September Mehemet Ali was defeated by the Turks, and Louis-Philippe made it clear that France was going to back down. Throughout the crisis, radical politicians were supported in their attitude by a number of well-known intellectuals, including Quinet,[4] who preached war as a means of national regeneration.

If close observers of this country agree on any one thing it is on recognizing several signs which mark the wasting away of society. Yet France does not believe she is dying. She laughs at her prophets. . . .

During the Restoration, France was throttled by invasion and taken prisoner of war, but she did not accept the violence that was done to her. She was overpowered but she was not resigned. Her might was vanquished but not her spirit. After 1830, however, when the same international agreements still existed, it appeared that France accepted her servitude, agreed to her downfall and voluntarily placed the seal on her defeat. What had seemed up to now an act of violence took the name of legality, for by this free adherence the whole of a nation became, in appearance, the accomplice of its own ruin. . . . With the country keeping the enemy's knife in its wound and no longer dreaming of wrenching it out, the disease spread silently. Peace became as disastrous as war. The happy progress of industry and agriculture made people forget that these riches covered death. . . .

The principle of internal liberty has been achieved, but we lack the external independence needed to exercise it. The nation is at one and the same time triumphant and broken. Free, and held in an iron grip; free, and astonished at not being able to move; free, and unable to breathe. Because in its relations with neighbouring states the government meets everywhere this legacy of defeat, this obstacle hampering it

[4] Edgar Quinet (1803-75) was already well-known in literate circles for his atheism, revealed in his commentary (1838) on Strauss's Life of Jesus. He was also an authority on the history and politics of Germany, where he had lived for some years. In 1841 he became professor of literature at the Collège de France, whether he launched an attack on the Jesuits.

at every turn, one soon comes to believe that the government is to blame and that it alone is the source of all the evil. Vainly one cries to it to hold its head high, without thinking that the country drags the length of its chain at its feet. In this state of triumphant powerlessness a dull fury gradually takes possession of people: the feebleness of the State gives birth to a thousand sects which mutually devour each other. Many people, losing their ancient respect for their country, lose their respect for themselves at the same time. Others, who are more energetic and would have been capable of public service if there had been anything to serve beyond a phantom, throw themselves feverishly into the pursuit of private fortune and insolently proclaim themselves kings of this dead society. . . .

If this is the situation within the country, it is far worse without. As long as the nation which has submitted to defeat attempts nothing serious, its conquerors agree to let it think that it has recovered. But the day that it wishes to re-assert itself and play a part in important matters, the dependence to which it has been reduced and which it has accepted brutally makes itself felt. That is what has happened to France today. She could indulge in the belief that the treaties of 1815 were at least half effaced as long as she was occupied with secondary matters. Antwerp and Ancona helped to delude her in this respect.[5] She was allowed to cherish her illusions when there was nothing decisive at the root of her policy, but as soon as the important question of the East blew up, enveloping and absorbing all others, the veils fell off. The frightful reality of international law founded on invasion reappeared; the bonds of 1815 were suddenly tightened again. . . .

That is the evil, and it is deep-rooted. It is for you to decide if you wish to cure it, for here the will is the sovereign remedy. I do not know, though, if you have reflected enough on what war could mean for this country. . . . Are you determined, seriously and irrevocably, to perish to the last man rather than to endure defeat once more? Are you prepared to make each of your cities a French Saragossa if need be?[6] Will the word 'capitulation' be effaced from the language as long as success is uncertain on your side? Do you feel the earth shake under your feet and feel in your hearts the strength necessary to multiply that of the nation tenfold? Will you know how to support not so much the heat of combat as the loss of your property and your everyday comforts?

[5] In February 1832, when the Austrians occupied Bologna to 'protect' the Pope, the French occupied Ancona on the same pretext. In October of the same year a French army besieged Antwerp, freed it from the Dutch, and then withdrew.

[6] Sarragossa was famed for the devotion and fanaticism displayed by the citizens when the town was besieged during the Peninsular War.

Above all will parties and factions sign a truce for a moment, and will
that old word patriotism, which no-one dares to pronounce any more,
speak again to the hearts of men? If so, invoke your rights and embrace
war. Save France! Save the future! Save all that perishes!

> Edgar Quinet, *1815 et 1840* (Paris, Sept. 1840).
> From *Oeuvres complètes* (Paris, 1858) vol. X

4 Bonapartism

(a) *Napoleonic ideas*

The Napoleonic pretender, Louis Napoleon Bonaparte (nephew of the great
Emperor), was well aware that militarism was more or less confined to the
radical populations of a few large towns. The majority of Frenchmen, small
peasant proprietors, were averse to war. In a pamphlet published whilst in exile
in London in 1839 he argued that Bonapartism stood for glory through democracy rather than through war. The pamphlet sold half a million copies in
France before 1848.

The Emperor Napoleon did more than anyone else to accelerate the
reign of liberty, by saving the moral influence of the Revolution and
diminishing the fears that it inspired. Without the Consulate and
Empire the Revolution would have been nothing more than a great
drama which left behind fine memories but few traces. The revolution
would have been swamped in counter-revolution. But the contrary
happened, because Napoleon planted in France and introduced everywhere in Europe the principle benefits of the great crisis of '89 and
because, to use his own words, he 'cleansed the Revolution, strengthened the kings, and ennobled the people'. He cleansed the Revolution by
separating the truths which it had caused to triumph from the passions
whose raging had obscured them. He strengthened the kings by
making power once more honoured and respectable. He ennobled the
people by making them aware of their strength and giving them the
kind of institutions which raise men in their own estimation. . . .
    To be capable of accomplishing such a task, your very substance must
respond to that of the people. You must feel as they do, and your interests must be so fused with theirs that you and they can but triumph
or fall together. It was this unity of thought, feeling and will that made
up the entire strength of the Emperor. . . .
    Napoleon was the supreme head of the state, the elect of the people,
the representative of the nation. In his public actions the Emperor

always prided himself on owing everything to the French people. . . .
To sum up the imperial system, one could say that the base was
democratic, since all power came from the people, whilst its organization was hierarchical, since there were various ranks in society to
stimulate every kind of ability. Competition was open to 40 million
people. Merit alone was the distinguishing feature, and the different
degrees in the social scale were the reward. . . .

The aim which he came so near to fulfilling, in spite of the complexity
of events and the continual conflict of opposing interests, was to assure
the independence of France and establish a sound European peace. The
more one unravels the secrets of diplomacy the more one is convinced
that Napoleon was led on step by step, by force of circumstances, towards that gigantic empire which was created by war and destroyed by
war. He was not an aggressor. On the contrary he was obliged all the
time to repulse European coalitions.

Once Napoleonic Europe had been founded, Napoleon would have
gone on to establish peacetime institutions in France. He would have
consolidated liberty: he needed only to fill in the lines which he had
sketched. The government of Napoleon could have supported liberty
better than any other, for the simple reason that it would have strengthened his throne whilst overthrowing thrones which were not securely
founded. Liberty would have confirmed Napoleon's power because he
had established in France all the pre-requisites of liberty; because his
power rested on the entire mass of the nation; because his interests were
the same as those of the people and because perfect confidence reigned
between the governing and the governed. . . .

In conclusion may I repeat that the Napoleonic idea is not an idea of
war but a social idea – an industrial, commercial, humanitarian idea. If
to some men it always seems to be surrounded by the thunder of
combat, this is because it was indeed enveloped for too long in the
smoke of cannon and the dust of battle. But today the clouds have
vanished, and one can see beyond the glory of arms a civil glory which
was greater and more lasting.

> Prince Napoleon-Louis Bonaparte, *Des Idées*
> *napoléoniennes* (Paris 1839) pp. 19, 20, 21, 107,
> 121, 145, 179–80, 200

(b) *A bonapartist manifesto*

On 6 August 1840 Louis-Napoleon landed at Wimereux with 56 men, 9 horses
and a tame vulture, and attempted to raise the garrison at Boulogne. The
following extract is translated from a leaflet distributed by Louis-Napoleon's

followers on entering Boulogne. The attempted *coup* failed and the whole party were arrested while trying to swim back to the paddle steamer which had brought them from England. Louis-Napoleon was tried by the Chamber of Peers and sentenced to life imprisonment in the fortress of Ham. He escaped in 1846 and fled to England.

Frenchmen! The ashes of the Emperor must return only to a regenerated France.[7] The shade of the great man must not be sullied by impure and hypocritical homage. Glory and liberty must stand beside the tomb of Napoleon. Traitors to the country must away!

What have those who govern France done to deserve your affection? They promised you peace and they gave you civil war and a disastrous war in Africa; they promised you reduced taxes, and all the gold you possess will not satisfy their greed. They promised you honest government and they reign only by corruption; they promised you liberty and they protect only privileges and abuses. They oppose all reform and promote only arbitrariness and anarchy. They promised stability and in ten years they have stabilized nothing. Above all they promised that they would conscientiously defend our honour, our rights, and our interests, and at every point they have sold our honour, abandoned our rights and betrayed our interests! It is time to put a stop to such iniquities, time to be asking them what they have done with the great, generous, unanimous France of 1830.

Farmers! They have left you in peacetime with heavier taxes than Napoleon levied during the war. Industrialists and businessmen! Your interests have been sacrificed to the demands of foreigners, and the money that the Emperor used to encourage and enrich you has been employed in corruption. Lastly all you poor and labouring classes, refuge of all the noble sentiments in France, do you not remember that it was from among you that Napoleon chose his lieutenants, his marshals, his ministers, his princes, and his friends? Give me your co-operation and let us show the world that you and I have not changed.

I had hoped, like you, that we could have corrected the evil influences of the government without revolution, but today there is no longer any hope of that. Ministries have changed ten times in ten years, and they could change ten times more and the ills and miseries of the country would remain the same.

When one has the honour to be at the head of such a nation as the French, there is one infallible method of achieving great things, and

---

[7] Louis-Philippe's third son, the Duc de Joinville, had set sail from France on 7 July to bring Napoleon's ashes back from St. Helena.

that is to will them. In France today there is nothing but violence on the one hand and licence on the other. My aim is to re-establish order and liberty. My aim is, by surrounding myself with all the top people in every sphere in the country and by relying solely on the will and interest of the masses, to found an unshakable edifice. My aim is to give France genuine alliances and a firm peace, not to throw her into the hazards of largescale war.

Frenchmen! I see before me a brilliant future for the country. I sense behind me the shade of the Emperor driving me onward, and I shall not stop till I have taken up once more the sword of Austerlitz, restoring the eagle to the standard and justice to the people.

Long live France!
Signed, Napoleon
Gazette des Tribunaux, 9 August 1840

5   The Napoleonic legend

(a) *The return of Napoleon's ashes*

On 15 December 1840 the remains of Napoleon I, brought back from St. Helena by permission of the British government, were ceremonially interred in the Invalides, where they became an object of popular pilgrimage. This is how a workingman's newspaper, the *Atelier*, reported the event.

This imposing ceremony, so impatiently awaited by all classes of the population in Paris, was a subject of fear and anxiety to our rulers. Napoleon, though dead, still frightened them. Consequently the illustrious captive came back to us escorted like a prisoner of war, for one could not describe in any other way the official reception our statesmen had arranged for him. . . .

People grasp a situation pretty well when it is presented to them in a concrete form, and they saw the shameful peace régime obliged to render hypocritical hommage to the greatest of all representatives of French honour, to the punctilious plenipotentiary of the French Republic, to the man who preferred to abdicate and renounce the throne rather than agree to a peace which would be called positively glorious today. The most bitter reflections on past and present dawned upon that immense crowd which had gathered to commemorate both Republic and Empire in the person of their most vigorous representative.

It was not the restorer of the nobility, the resurrector of the categories of the old régime, or the ambitious conqueror that the crowd came to salute, but the artillery lieutenant of '93, the victor of Arcoli and the Pyramids, the general who commanded the campaign of France in 1814 and sought death on the battlefield of Waterloo. It was also the prisoner of St. Helena, the heroic victim of England, expiating on a rock the victories of France. Above all it was revolutionary France, represented at this ceremony by the veterans of the armies of the Republic and Empire, that the people of Paris came to salute, touched by all these memories of our glorious past. . . .

Oh yes, it was a fine occasion, the 15th of December. It was neither a funeral nor a memorial service, as the official programme chose to call it, but the glorification of France great and honoured, the apotheosis of the France of the Revolution and at the same time the most scathing rejection of the cowardly policy which abandoned Italy, Belgium, Poland and Egypt! Worthy Ministers, you did not attend this ceremony. You dared not appear before your sovereign judge. . . . If you had joined the procession you would have heard the formidable cry, 'Down with traitors!' But the reports of your police must have informed you of the universal reprobation you excite, for all Paris took part in the demonstration.

You thought you would do a bit of play-acting, but your pretence at a warlike humour convinced no-one. You were mistaken if you thought you could amuse the nation with military fêtes when Austria is calling upon you to disarm. Your hopes have been cruelly shattered if you thought to make the people gathered round this tomb condone or forget your past actions.

Atelier, December 1840

(b) *A school book*

A popular reading book for use in schools, first published in 1846 and running to a second edition by 1848, instructed children in a romanticised version of Napoleon's career. The book took the form of question and answer between pupil and teacher.

Johnnie: Who was the greatest of all the kings of France, sir?

Teacher: It is difficult to say. I have already mentioned Charlemagne. . . . Alongside him one could place Louis XIV. . . . But there was a third; one whom I have seen myself. I have heard his voice; I have stood on guard outside his tent. I can still see his small white hands, and his eyes shining as he passed us in review. We loved him so much, we men of his generation, that we can hardly bear to speak of him. I mean

Napoleon. At first he was a simple artillery officer. He became a general, then First Consul of the French Republic, and finally Emperor of the French and King of Italy. He earned all these titles by his victories and by the good that he did to our country. He held out against all Europe leagued against him, and won the biggest and most terrible battles that had been fought for centuries. He put France on top again. . . . The benefits of the Revolution, which had been bought at the price of so much blood, would probably have been lost for ever if Napoleon had not come to power. He began by re-establishing our sacred religion, which had been abolished. He caused order and justice to reign every-where, restored plenty, allowed exiles to return, put into full force the new laws that the Revolution had been made for, and became through his innumerable victories one of the greatest warriors the world has ever seen.

Johnnie: In that case, how is it that his reign came to an end?

Teacher: All the kings of Europe, who resented his superiority, united against him. At the same time the French, who were tired of waging war continuously, began to serve him less zealously. In spite of this, his valour and genius enabled him to carry on for a while a fearful struggle against armies four times the strength of his own. But at last he was vanquished in 1815, in a disastrous battle called the battle of Waterloo. Then, although the English had always been his enemies he counted on their generosity, knowing that they would have been able to rely on his, and he gave himself up into their hands. He was mistaken, and it will be an eternal blot upon the honour of the English people that they betrayed his noble-hearted trust. Instead of giving him the hospitality he requested they took him to the island of St. Helena, which is nothing but a mass of barren rocks in the middle of the ocean, two thousand miles away from Europe. There he was shut up in a house that was uncomfortable and unhealthy, and watched closely, like a malefactor, whenever he wanted to go out; and the governor of the island, who had no respect for the misfortune of so great a man, tormented him until his death with petty acts of spitefulness.

Charles Jeannel, *Petit-Jean* (2nd ed., Paris 1848)
pp. 279–83

XI

PRIMARY EDUCATION

1 Provision of schools

As long ago as 1793 the Jacobin Declaration of the Rights of Man had declared education to be the need of all. Yet by 1828 it was reckoned that, out of 5½ million children between the ages of 6 and 15, 4 millions did not attend any school. The Charter of 1830 promised that there would be a law on education: the promise was carried out when Guizot became Minister of Education in the cabinet of 11 October 1832.

Act for the organization of primary education, 28 June 1833:

Article 4. Any person over the age of 18 shall be allowed to become a primary schoolteacher and direct any kind of primary school simply by presenting first, to the mayor of the commune in which he wishes to keep a school:

(a) a certificate of ability, obtained by examination, in accordance with the standard of school he wishes to establish.

(b) a certificate stating that the applicant is of a suitable character to engage in teaching. This certificate shall be granted, on the testimony of three municipal councillors, by the mayor of the commune or of each commune in which the candidate has resided during the past three years. . . .

Article 9. Every commune is obliged, either by itself or in conjunction with one or more neighbouring communes, to maintain at least one elementary primary school. . . .[1]

Article 10. Communes which are the chief town of a department or which have a population of more than 6,000 shall also have a superior primary school.

[1] The law made the interesting innovation of dividing primary education into two classes, elementary and superior.

Article 11. Each department, either by itself or in conjunction with one or more neighbouring departments, shall be obliged to maintain a teacher's training college. . . .

Article 12. Every schoolmaster employed by the commune shall be provided with:
  (a) a building suitably arranged for him to live in and receive scholars.
  (b) a fixed salary of not less than 200 francs for an elementary primary school and not less than 400 francs for a superior primary school.

Article 13. Where there are no endowments, gifts or bequests from which to provide a building and a salary in accordance with the preceding article, the municipal council shall decide on the necessary measures. Where the ordinary revenues are insufficient to establish elementary and superior primary schools, they shall be provided by means of a special tax voted by the municipal council (or, in default of such a vote, established by royal ordinance). . . .

Article 14. Pupils of the commune, or group of communes, who are designated by the municipal councils as unable to pay a fee shall be admitted free of charge to the elementary school. In the superior primary schools a number of free places, determined by the municipal council, may be reserved for children who pass an examination and who come from families which cannot pay fees.

Article 17. For each communal school there shall be a local supervisory committee consisting of the mayor or his deputy as president, the priest or pastor, and one or more well known citizens from the committee of the arrondissement. In communes where the population is divided between different denominations recognized by the state, the priest or the most senior of the priests and one minister from each of the other denominations (chosen by his consistory) shall sit on the communal supervisory committee. . . .

Article 18. Each arrondissement in the sub-prefecture shall have a special committee to control and encourage primary education. . . .

Article 19. The arrondissement committees shall consist of:
  The mayor of the chief town. . . .
  The J.P. or the most senior of the J.P.s. . . .
  The priest or the most senior of the priests. . . .
  One minister from each of the other denominations. . . .
  A headmaster, college principal, professor or dean, chosen by the

Minister of Public Instruction, wherever there is a college or similar institution in the area covered by the committee;

A primary school teacher residing in the area covered by the committee, chosen by the Minister of Public Instruction;

Three members of the council of the arrondissement. . . .

Such members of the general council of the department as live in the area covered by the committee.

The prefect shall preside, ex-officio, over all the committees in the department, and the sub-prefect over those in the arrondissement. The king's attorney shall be a member, ex-officio, of all arrondissment committees.

Article 21. The communal committee shall inspect all public and private schools in the commune. It shall see to the sanitary condition of the schools and the maintenance of discipline. . . . It shall see that the free education of poor children has been provided for. . . . In cases of emergency, and at the request of the communal committee, the mayor may provisionally suspend a teacher from his duties, reporting the suspension and the reasons for it within 24 hours to the arrondissement committee. . . .

Article 22. The arrondissement committee shall inspect, or if necessary arrange for delegates from among its own members or from outside to inspect all primary schools in its area. . . . It shall send a report each year to the prefect and the Minister of Public Instruction on the state of the primary schools in its area. . . . It shall appoint the communal schoolmasters.

M. Gréard, *La législation de l'instruction
primaire en France de 1789 jusqu'à nos jours*
(3 vol. Paris 1874) i, 236–45

2   What to teach

Guizot was as much concerned with the content of education as with the provision of schools. A decree issued by the Royal Council for Public Instruction on 25 April 1834 regulated teaching in primary schools as follows:

Article 2. To be admitted to an elementary school a child must be no less than 6 years old and no more than 13. . . .

Article 3. Every elementary school shall be divided into three principal divisions according to the age of the pupils and the subjects to be taught.

Article 4. Moral and religious instruction shall have first place in every division. Every class shall begin and end with prayers. Verses of Holy Scripture shall be learnt every day. Every Saturday the gospel for Sunday shall be recited. On Sundays and Feast Days the pupils shall be taken to Divine Service. . . . Where schools are frequented by children belonging to different denominations recognised by law, special measures shall be taken to see that the pupils receive the religious instruction their parents wish them to be given.

Article 5. Children aged 6 to 8 shall form the first division. In addition to reading out loud from religious books, they shall be particularly required to recite prayers. At the same time they shall be taught reading, writing, and the beginnings of mental arithmetic.

Article 6. Children aged 6 to 10 shall form the second division. Moral and religious instruction shall consist of Bible history from the Old and New Testaments. The children shall continue to practise reading, writing, and mental arithmetic. They shall also be taught written arithmetic and French grammar.

Article 7. Children from 10 years old to the time when they leave school shall form the third division. They shall make a special study of Christian doctrine. They shall continue to practise reading, writing, arithmetic and French grammar; in addition they shall be taught elementary geography and history, especially the geography and history of France. Where singing and drawing are taught, they should be placed for preference in this division. . . .

Article 16. Every Saturday the pupils shall recite what they have learnt during the week. The master may choose a certain number of pupils to help him, each one hearing five or six others. . . .

Article 17. Twice a year there shall be a general examination in the presence of members of the local committee, joined if desired by a member of the arrondissement committee. At the end of the examination a list of pupil's names shall be drawn up in order of merit and posted up in the schoolroom. . . .

Article 29. Pupils shall never be beaten. The only punishments authorized are the following:
One or more black marks;
Reprimand;
Surrender of one or more good conduct tickets;
Keeping in for a part or the whole of playtime, with a special task;

Kneeling during a part of schooltime or playtime;
Obligation to wear a notice specifying the offence;
Temporary expulsion from school.

M. Gréard, *op. cit.*, I, 317-24

3 Early reports

In 1837 a summary was published of the reports so far sent to the Minister of Education from 490 inspectors of schools.

Nothing gives a better idea of the suspicion with which primary education is generally viewed in France than the small number of buildings erected specially for the purpose. Some communes are fortunate in that the municipal council, when granting a hall to a schoolmaster, makes no other condition than that he should let them use it on the day of their sitting, or simply that he should let the tax-collector have an office and keep his accounts there. There are others where the place chosen for the classroom witnesses the man who is the schoolteacher in the morning mounting guard during the night, after presiding, as local fiddler, over a village dance in the evening; for the classroom has the three-fold privilege of being at one and the same time a school, a guard-room and a dance hall.

It is quite a rare phenomenon to see the schoolmaster allotting a separate room in his building for domestic purposes. . . . The classroom is not only his kitchen but his bedroom; indeed it constitutes his entire living quarters. If some member of his family is ill, say his wife or his daughter, or if something keeps them in bed rather later than usual, there is nothing else to do, I am afraid, but modestly to draw the curtains. In truth I do not know whether, from the point of view of morality, especially in schools composed of both boys and girls, it would not be better to have them living with the family pig and other domestic animals, as happens in several communes in the Saône-et-Loire, rather than have them assisting in the mistress's toilet and the feeding of the baby. . . .

One sometimes sees schoolmasters voluntarily seeking stables and cowsheds in which to hold their classes, in the hope of profiting from the heat which the beasts give off. . . . Sometimes schools are held in damp barns, low basements, cellars where one is obliged to climb down a ladder, unbelievably tiny places. . . .

In many places it is impossible to find a single man who can read, write and count. When a lawyer is called in to sign a document he takes care to arrive escorted by two permanent witnesses whom he has brought from the town, because he knows very well that he would search the area in vain for French citizens who could write their name. ... Communes are often for this reason greatly embarrassed when it comes to choosing a mayor. ... The examples cited are sufficient to prove the extent to which ignorance still reigns undisputed over the countryside, and the little reliance one can place on the help of certain authorities in stimulating the zeal of children and their families when their own lack of education makes them incapable of appreciating it or pointing out its advantages. ...

The forms which the general apathy takes are not even very varied. All the fine arguments put forward in different places, from north to south, boil down in the end to the following axioms: 'The children shall be what their fathers were. The sun shines equally on the ignorant and the learned.' Often, too, opposition comes from people who are quite exalted in their area. ... Sometimes they put it forward in the interests of agriculture: when all the children of the neighbourhood can read and write, where shall we find labourers? ... Sometimes farmers who are slightly well-to-do revolt out of a stupid pride at the idea of sending their children to sit on the same bench as the poor. ... It is not just that they fear the influence of bad habits and dangerous principles contracted in the midst of poverty, but that they are indignant at the thought of education levelling out the difference between wealth and poverty. To be able to read, write and count is for them a symbol of wealth, like being able to ride to market on a pony whilst the poor plod along beside them on foot. ...

In most parts of France, school is not attended for more than three months in the year. (This is the average, taken for convenience, between areas where the children attend for four or five months and those where two months a year are said to be enough to educate them.) All the rest of the year, from the ages of 8 to 10, they follow their fathers in the fields, and exhaust their young bodies in work which is often beyond their strength. ... What is the result? Since they have forgotten in the interval the little that they learnt before, since their hands, from being burdened with field work and the weight of the hoe, have become calloused and almost numb and are not supple enough to make the strokes, since the rough language they have heard for nine months has made them forget a more civilized tongue, they must start again; and one cannot reckon at less than a month the time needed to regain all that has been lost. This leaves barely two months. One must remember, too, that it is the time of year when the days are shortest, the roads at their worst, and illness most frequent. If school begins at 8 a.m. the children who live in the village may perhaps get there, but those who live on some distant farm lose precious time on the journey. In the afternoon they have to be let out early so as not to be overtaken by darkness or wild beasts. . . .

Among the special reasons put forward here and there for opposing education we would mention in the Jura the habit of employing children at a very early age to go out selling fruit, oil and wine in the mountains, and in the Cantal the annual migration of children who are sent to beg or sweep chimneys in the town. Elsewhere it is basket-making, weaving, needlework or knitting that occupies the children and takes them away from school. But of all the jobs on which they are commonly employed the most unfortunate is probably that of minding the herds, the flocks and the geese. It is then, when they are away from their families, left to their own thoughts and to all the mischievous desires that idleness prompts, that they lose such precious time. . . .

The law demands that 'moral and religious instruction, reading, writing, elements of the French language, arithmetic, and weights and measures' be taught in elementary schools. . . . The masters found in charge of schools do not so much as approach this degree of education, modest though it is. I believe they can all read, with the pronunciation more or less correct, though some are good and others bad and the standard of diction varies. I am assured that they cannot all write, and that among those who claim to possess this accomplishment there are a lot of semi-literates who are not capable of correcting their pupils. . . .

When we made a general round of primary education in 1833 [we found that] the teacher was often regarded in the commune as being on the same footing as a beggar. Between the shepherd and him, the preference was for the shepherd, and when the mayors (whom God knows, in the countryside, hardly belong to the aristocracy) wanted to show friendliness towards the schoolteacher they made him eat in the kitchen. Many teachers did not make enough to live on. . . . In many places they were never paid in cash: each family put aside the worst part of their produce to give to the schoolmaster when he came round to the doors on Sunday with his sack on his back. . . . Even today when the law, to guarantee them a more honest existence, requires that they be given a minimum salary of 200 francs, you cannot imagine the conditions that are invented to make them lose the benefit of it. . . . They are made to dig graves, or act as town crier, or clean out the public lavatories. . . . And what can one say about the other professions in which schoolmasters engage in order to supplement their modest income! The shops adjoining the classroom, which allow the schoolmaster to leave a dictation or recital of the cathechism to go and sell tobacco to the customers or wine by the glass; the schools where the teacher is a shoemaker or blacksmith or carpenter or cooper, and deafens the children with the sound of his hammer. . . etc.

P. Lorain, *Tableau de l'Instruction primaire en France* (Paris, 1837) pp. 1-4, 13-23, 57, 60-67

XII

SOCIAL SURVEYS

1 The industrial north

During the reign of Louis-Philippe 'the condition of the people question' began
to agitate the public conscience much as it did in England. A number of surveys
were made, not, as in England, by parliamentary commissions but by serious
minded individuals. Viscount Alban de Villeneuve-Bargemont (1784-1850),
one of the precursors of Christian Socialism, belonged to an aristocratic family
which had stayed in France during the Revolution and served both Napoleon
and the restored Bourbons as able administrators. After being dismissed from
his post as prefect of the Nord in 1830, Alban used his enforced leisure to write a
vast treatise on the conditions he had witnessed. He believed that the only
remedy for the evils of 'the new feudalism' created by the rise of capitalism was
the re-ordering of society on truly Christian principles with the government
intervening to see that food and goods were properly distributed and that industry concentrated on producing necessaries rather than luxuries.

The territory of the department of the Nord is cultivated to perfection.
Industry has made tremendous progress there, especially since 1814. . . .
One can without exaggeration compare it in this respect with Belgium
Switzerland, and even in some ways with England, whose ideas about
industrial economy it has adopted. By a necessary analogy, however,
this department, which France can proudly rate as one of Louis XIV's
finest acquisitions, is also the portion of the kingdom which contains the
largest number of paupers; just as England, the Low Countries and
Switzerland are the areas of Europe where pauperism is most widespread
and deep-rooted.

The returns made by order of the administrative authorities in 1828
furnished proof that in the department of the Nord there were 163,453
persons listed as paupers on the registers of the welfare committees;
that is, rather more than a sixth of the total population. . . . This number does not include 800 sick, 2,529 old people, and 1,332 orphans,
making a total of 4,667 persons maintained in hospitals; nor does it

include 3,000 foundlings. This mass of paupers is composed chiefly of:
1. industrial workers who cannot keep their families on their wages and are thrown entirely into dependence on public and private charity in the event of sickness, scarcity or unemployment;
2. agricultural workers with too many children, who are without means during the off-season;
3. workers without education, without foresight and without economy, brutalized by drink or debilitated by industrial labour, who have reached middle age without any savings and are no longer in a fit state to provide fully for their families by working, especially as their families are nearly always large;
4. old people, prematurely senile, who are abandoned by their children, who have not been able to get into hospital and who cannot be properly looked after by the welfare committees;
5. children and orphans too young to work for a living, a large number of whom, stricken with infirmities or incurably crippled, are a permanent charge upon their parents and communes;
6. lastly, a large number of families who are hereditary paupers or beggars, without training, without intelligence, without energy either physical or moral, living in towns, herded into dark, damp cellars or into attics exposed to all the rigours of the seasons; the majority adding the most disgusting immorality to the sad list of infirmities transmitted from father to son. . . .

The desire for strong liquor is such, among the working classes in the towns, that fathers and often mothers of families pawn their belongings in order to satisfy it, and even sell the clothes off their backs, put there by public charity or individual kindness. The municipal pawn shops opened at Lille, Cambrai, Douai, Bergues and Valenciennes, far from alleviating the poverty of the people, merely hasten their demoralization and their undoing.

Religious teaching has great difficulty in making any headway in the midst of all this brutishness; worthy members of the clergy are given little or no hearing. Besides, the small number of priests in the diocese cannot cater for such widespread need, especially as it would require some sort of daily and permanent care for each family.

It will readily be understood that the majority of welfare departments, being powerless to alleviate wretchedness so deep and inveterate, are afraid of making any new efforts at amelioration in case they should be unsuccessful and thereby antagonise large numbers of people who are a prey to all the horrors of want. This kind of job is little sought after. To carry it out with real devotion requires religious feeling strong enough to brave all the distasteful and even dangerous situations which accompany it. Such a degree of virtue is rarer than charity, which confines itself to giving. One finds oneself, more often than not, obliged to rely on officious agents for the distribution of relief. Under the name of *pauvrisseurs* they hand over money direct, or bread vouchers as they think fit, in accordance with lists of paupers which they can draw up themselves without supervision. It is only in a very small number of parishes that nuns or charitable ladies distribute relief to the poor and sick in their homes. . . .

It is above all in the capital of the department, Lille, that one is continually presented with the most fearful combination of every kind of misery. In 1828, out of a population of 23,381 paupers there were 3,687 living in underground cellars, without fresh air or light, and given over to the most disgusting squalor. Father, mother, children and sometimes grown-up brothers and sisters slept in the same wretched bed. . . . It is understandable that in such difficult circumstances habits should become excessively corrupt. Outrageous immorality is seen every day. People marry young, and illegitimate unions are numerous. A large part of the population lives on theft. Begging is carried on publicly by huge bands of beggars who alarm the few property owners. There is nothing one can do to destroy this nuisance. Indeed it is impossible not to tolerate it in a situation where one can neither provide work and adequate wages for the able-bodied poor nor relief and shelter for the wretches who cannot work.

A. de Villeneuve-Bargemont, *Économie politique chrétienne* (3 vols., Paris, 1834) ii, 51, 53-4, 60-64

2   Public health

In 1835 the Academy of Moral and Political Sciences commissioned a doctor, Louis René Villermé (1782-1863), to carry out investigations into the health of workers. He decided to concentrate on those industries, outside Paris, which employed the most hands; i.e. the textile industries. His account of working and living conditions in the large cotton towns of Haut-Rhin, especially Mulhouse, soon became famous.

At Mulhouse, Dornach, etc., the spinning and weaving sheds open as a rule at 5 o'clock in the morning and close at 8 o'clock at night, or sometimes nine. . . . During this time there is an hour and a half off for dinner and an hour for tea. . . .

The price of lodgings does not always allow those cotton operatives who draw the smallest wages or who have the heaviest commitments to lodge near their workshops. This is particularly the case at Mulhouse. The town is growing rapidly, but industry is developing faster still, and it is not possible to take in all the people who are continually being attracted to the town by the need for work. Hence it is necessary for the poorest, who in any case could not pay for lodgings at the price they are, to go and live a long way out of the town – a mile, a mile and a half, or even further – and consequently to do two or three miles to get to work in the morning and return home at night.

The workshops of Mulhouse alone, in 1835, contained more than 5,000 workers who lodged in the villages round about. These are the least well paid workers. They mostly consist of poor families with a lot of young children. . . . One should see them arriving in the town each morning and leaving at night. Among them are large numbers of thin, pale women, walking barefoot through the sludge, wearing their aprons or their skirts over their heads to shield their faces and shoulders when it rains, since they haven't got umbrellas; and a still larger number of young children, equally dirty and haggard, dressed in rags which are thick with oil that has fallen on them whilst working. The children are better protected from the rain by the impermeability of their clothing, but they do not even carry a basket with food for the day like the women I have just described. They carry in their hands, or hidden in their clothing as best they can, a piece of bread which has to last them until they go home.

. . . It is understandable that others, to avoid tramping so far twice a day, should herd into quarters which, though cramped and unhealthy, are at least close to their work. I have seen these wretched lodgings in Mulhouse, Dornoch, and neighbouring towns, with two families sleeping in opposite corners of the room on straw placed on the flag-stones and held in by two planks. Some scraps of blanket and a filthy mattress of feathers are often all that cover the straw. . . .

In the families of cotton weavers and spinners a half of the children die before the age of two. What must this mean in the way of lack of care, neglect on the part of the parents, privation and suffering?

L. R. Villermé, *Tableau de l'État physique et moral des ouvriers employés dans les manufactures de coton, de laine, et de soie* (2 vols., Paris, 1840)

I, 14, 21-29

Though less famous than the account of Mulhouse, Villermé's descriptions of smaller towns were more typical of industry as a whole in France.

The town of Saint-Quentin was once a centre for the manufacture of linen, which had a wide market; but this has been gradually ruined over the past twenty years or so by the growth of cheap cotton. . . . The spinning of cotton is concentrated in the town, but that of linen still occupies women in the country districts, particularly during the long winter evenings. As for weaving, both of cotton and linen, this is carried on almost exclusively in the villages; and since the cloth made with the two threads is manufactured in exactly the same way and on the same looms the same workers make it alternately. Each year, for the four or five months of the harvest, these weavers devote themselves entirely to agriculture. Most of them own the house that they live in, and a garden, and many have, besides, a small field which they cultivate and which stands them in good stead when they cannot get enough wages by weaving.

The cloth is either manufactured for a merchant, who provides the materials, agrees in advance on the cost of the labour and pays for it when the goods are finished, or the weaver works for himself. In the latter case the weaver buys the thread and when he has finished the cloth he takes it to the town to sell it to a merchant for what he can get, or else he sells it at home to a middleman, that is to an agent who goes round the villages or who lives on the spot. . . .

The hand weavers who are also farmers and who own the house they live in (that is, the comfortably off weavers) have almost always fair-sized homes, clean and decent; the others have only small ones, badly kept and miserably furnished, where the whole family, often composed of five or six persons – husband, wife, and three or four children – usually sleep in the same room. It should be added that the living quarters of the latter leave much to be desired compared with their dress, for frequently among them it is a case of who can out-do the others in elegance and pretentiousness, especially on Sundays. . . .

It is chiefly women and children who are employed in factories in the town. For cheapness the poorest of them live several in one room, where they sleep on wretched beds, a fact which does not stop them, however, particularly the young ones, from being smartly dressed. This taste for clothes, this love of extravagance among the young ones, combined with the communal bedrooms and the mixing of sexes in the workshops, relaxes and depraves standards. Foremen and ordinary workmen have assured me that no attempt is made to keep a watch on them in the workshops of Saint-Quentin; on the contrary, they say, boys and girls have complete freedom in their relationship with each other. . . . Saint-Quentin is not a large town, yet for the period 1825 to 1835 inclusive rather more than a fifth of all the births recorded in the registers were illegitimate. . . .

A family composed of four persons – husband, wife, a child starting work and another younger – spend between them on food alone 2 francs a day. Supposing they earn 3 francs, including Sundays; that leaves them only 20 sous for all their other expenses. If for some reason or other, which is easily imagined, their average income per day is less than 3 francs, they are unable to provide for their essential needs. In the towns the poorest workers, or the thriftiest ones, cut down on the expense of food each day as follows:

Coarse bread, costing 17½ sous per 8 livres . . . . 4½ sous
Thin soup, with beans, potatoes etc., or sometimes
    the cut-offs from the animals slaughtered at the
    butchers, or even a little pork . . . . 6 sous

——————
10½ sous
——————

But this saving can only be done at the cook-shops where one can go and get a meal a day, taking one's own bread. . . .

L. R. Villermé, *Tableau de l'État physique et
moral des ouvriers employés dans les manufactures
de coton, de laine, et de soie* (2 vols., Paris, 1840)
ii, 116-30

3   Statistics

In 1840 Eugène Buret (1810-42) was awarded a prize by the Academy of Political and Moral Sciences for a treatise comparing poverty among workers in England and France. One of the most important passages in the treatise was an attempt by Buret to arrive at statistics, not then a known science.

There are in France 1,329 hospitals and asylums for 40,000 communes. In 1833 these establishments admitted 425,029 persons belonging to the class of the very poor. In France the people who go into a hospital to die really are driven there by poverty. . . . The welfare committees, which distribute aid to recognised paupers in their homes, assisted 695,932 persons during the same year 1833. . . . The number of persons officially listed as paupers was, therefore, in 1833, 1,120,961; which gives a ratio of 1 official pauper in every 29·021 of the population. It is not difficult to see that this figure is only a fraction of the total. . . . With the exception of foundlings, who have only a mother, all these poor people have a family and consequently share with three or four other people – wives, aged parents and children – the usual privations of poverty and the more frightful experiences of extreme misery. Assuming that each official pauper represents at least three actual paupers, the number 1,120,961 assisted persons gives us a mass of human suffering which must amount to 1 in every 9·673 of the total population.

We have, however, a surer method of divining the approximate sum of pauperism in France, The documents of 1833 . . . reveal that, among the inmates of hospitals cited above, 45,303 persons died. If this number is multiplied in accordance with the death rate of the population (1 in 39) it is obvious that we shall obtain the probable number of paupers who need to go to hospital to seek the favour of a coffin. This calculation gives us a total of 1,766,717, or one pauper in 28·43 of the whole population. But the poor die quicker than wealthier sections of the population. . . . In the capital the average number of dead in proportion to the whole population is 1 in 36·44, but the ratio varies from one quarter to another according to the degree of wealth of the inhabitants. Thus in the 1st arrondissement it is only 1 in 52 inhabitants, whereas in the 7th, 8th and 12th arrondissements, which have chiefly working class populations swarming like bees in a hive, the proportion of dead rises to the level of 1 in 30, 1 in 28, and 1 in 26! . . . In order to calculate the number of miserable wretches from the lists of dead in the hospitals, let us take, then, a death rate above the average – for example that of the 12th arrondissement, where death strikes 1 in every 26 persons annually. This calculation gives us a total of 1,183,138 individuals who pay to the hospitals an annual toll of 45,303 dead. Compared to the total population of France this figure is in the ratio of 1 to 27·38. . . .

It should be noted, however, that the probable total of paupers (1,183,138) does not relate to the whole population of France. The vast majority of the inhabitants of the countryside, the agricultural nation, contribute hardly any recruits to the hospitals and welfare bureaux. The misery of the countryside, if its poverty merits the name, escapes all our calculations; it remains an unknown quantity. Only towns and boroughs with a population of more than 5,000 have hospitals and asylums, and these establishments are filled in large measure by inhabitants of the localities in which they are situated, plus a suburban area of about the same population. Now, the towns and boroughs with more than 5,000 inhabitants account for only 5,041,302 in the total population of France. On doubling this number, in order to take into account the paupers in the suburbs and neighbouring country districts which share in the charity of the hospitals, we arrive at about a third of the population of France. It is on this third alone that one should calculate the ratio of indigence to the population, since the other two thirds suffer and die at home, without receiving official aid. The number of paupers obtained above permits us to suppose that out of every 8·94 persons living in towns and boroughs in France, 1 is destined to die in a hospital.

Poverty grows along with the population, perhaps in the same proportion. It grows along with wealth, which throws it into relief and makes it conscious of itself by the painful effect of contrast. The more numerous the armies the bloodier the battles, and industry, in its present state, is a perpetual fight. The hospitals of the populous towns are like the ambulances which bring up the rear of large armies. . . .

It is impossible to define the extent of privation among the peasant poor. What may look to us like signs of the most abject misery – a habitation of wretched appearance, devoid of the equipment which renders life pleasant and comfortable, coarse food and ugly clothes—all that, to them, is only poverty, and poverty is not suffering. Even the most poverty-stricken of country workers, such as the vine-growers of the south, are not a prey to physical debility as distressing as that of the workers who compose the fighting battalions of industry. Moral suffering is unknown to them. Sad though it may be to owe exemption from suffering to ignorance of anything better, at least they escape the knowledge of poverty with all its humiliations; and after a life of hard toil, which is not without its pleasant days, they have as final consolation the happiness of being laid to rest under the green grass, along with their humble ancestors, in the blessed soil of the graveyard beside the church.

Eugène Buret, *De la misère des classes laborieuses en Angleterre et en France* (2 vols., Paris, 1840) i, 245–57

4 The criminal classes

Paris, like most capital cities of Europe, increased its population enormously during the 1830s and '40s. The people who herded together in the narrow alleys of these ancient cities were, for the most part, not industrial workers but journeymen and apprentices in the old crafts, small shop-keepers, hawkers, odd-jobmen, road-sweepers, rag-pickers and a host of others making ends meet. They furnished a fair number of petty criminals. The following extract is taken from a treatise written by an official of the prefecture of the Seine department and awarded a prize by the Institute.

The government has tried more than once to ascertain the real strength of the idle, wayward and depraved classes – i.e. of that section of the population which, in Paris and other large towns, forms the bedrock of all that is most abject, corrupt and dangerous to society. . . . It is generally agreed that the most dangerous elements of the vicious class are gamblers, prostitutes with their clients and bullies, keepers of brothels, vagabonds, swindlers, confidence tricksters, pick-pockets, thieves of both sexes and fences. . . .

The prostitutes are divided into two distinct classes: those registered at the prefecture of police, and those who are refractory or unregistered. The registered prostitutes form two categories: the isolated or free, and those attached to a brothel. The isolated ones are those who live in low-class furnished rooms or digs where they provide their own furniture. They form usually two-thirds of the prostitutes on the books. On 1 July 1836 the number of licensed brothels was 186 and the number of prostitutes registered had risen to 3,800. It was estimated that there were about 4,000 unregistered. . . . It is usual for the police to arrest a dozen or so of these girls each year and force them to be registered in the interests of public health. . . .

For convenience the word 'vagabond' has been restricted to that section of the poor who live aimlessly in the large towns and border on a state of mendicity because of the precarious life they lead. I have included, therefore, both adults who come under the above definition and those ragamuffin children who are without parents, or have been abandoned by their parents, or have deserted the parental roof, and who roam about the main centres of Paris living on what they can get from various commissions according to their age, or by furtive begging or taking to petty theft. The total number of these two sorts of vagabond is estimated at 1,500. This figure may at first appear too small when one thinks of the vast number of children habitually swarming about the markets and boulevards, but when one remembers that it signifies only the number of vagabonds included in the strict legal sense of the word one will perhaps decide that it is a reasonable estimate. . . .

Amongst the individuals who form the dangerous class, a good many have neither stick not stone. They form the regular occupants of those wretched haunts which will take in anybody, in the poorest quarters and most disgusting streets of the capital. The price paid in these places varies from 2 sous to 5 sous a night. The men who keep them are of two kinds. Some, a minority, only take people for the night; the others take bookings either for the night or for the week, month or even year. The number of these lodging houses, the most ill-famed of all, came to 243 on 1 July 1836. Together they contained a population of about 6,000, or about 24 occupants per house. Women living by prostitution or theft accounted for one-third. . . .

In trying to determine the strength of this class I have indicated the chief elements. These elements are scattered more or less in all quarters of Paris. The richest and most thickly populated are not exempt, since it is rare for even the handsomest quarters not to contain some narrow alley, lined with old houses, ill-looking and badly kept. It is in such places that the doss houses are set up, and the prostitutes, pimps, thieves and rogues congregate. Around them collect the gamblers, vagabonds, and all the rest who have no means of livelihood.

However, there are some quarters which these people seek out and frequent more readily than others, and among them one can single out a few which, because of their central position, seem to be the particular domain of prostitutes, vagabonds and above all malefactors. They include the Cité, Arcis, and Saint-Honoré. Whoever has visited the streets in these areas will not be surprised. Their narrow filthy alleys flanked by houses four storeys high, whose entrances never seem to have porters, have been abandoned to the most ill-famed and corrupt population of the capital. The Cité, especially, has a sinister aspect which contrasts strangely with the quays and monuments around and alongside it. It is traversed by roads eight feet wide at the very most and bordered by houses blackened by the weather. These tall houses, as I have said, make the streets dark and humid, and they are themselves badly lit, especially on the ground floor. Spirit shops, eating houses and gaming dens abound, and the gloominess of them, added to the repulsive appearance of the streets of the quarter, puts secret dread into the passer-by who has been led there by curiosity, knowing that most of these places are the habitual haunt of low prostitutes and of the bandits who lodge round about. The doss houses and brothels which harbour this section of the population are worthy by their filthiness of the streets and quarters where they are situated. . . .

In speaking of the hideous refuges known as cheap boarding houses I cannot resist trying to give a picture of some of them. . . . The most noticeable characteristic of all these houses is a degree of filth which makes them real breeding grounds of infection. There are some which, instead of beds, have only disgusting pallets; the rooms give on to corridors devoid of air and light; the sinks and lavatories on each floor give off a suffocating stench; the stairs are constantly damp and covered with slime which renders them almost unusable. . . . In others the courtyard is only four feet square and full of ordure. On to it open the bedrooms, which are crowded with people. The lavatories on the fifth floor overflow and the waste pours down the stairs, inundating them from top to bottom. Many of the rooms have no other opening than the door giving on to this staircase. The occupants are thieves, pickpockets, pimps, low-class prostitutes, and all that is most abject among mankind. In one of the houses the entire occupants sleep on rags picked up in the streets. The rags are piled up on the ground floor and given out to chance arrivals – beggars, organ grinders, casual prostitutes, Italians with performing animals, and pimps.

H. A. Frégier, *Des classes dangereuses de la population dans les grandes villes* (2 vols., Paris 1840) i, 47–8, 50–52, 134–6, 139–41

XIII

SOCIAL ATTITUDES AND THEORIES

1 Official attitudes

In 1839 nearly 150,000 children between the ages of 7 and 14 were working in the cotton industry alone. Petitions from philanthropic millowners and others led to some discussion of the problem in the Chambers, but nothing was done until 1841.

Minister of Finance:[1] There is no more distressing sight than that of the unfortunate children attached to a great many of the factories in France. All the disadvantages that the petition has brought to our notice... are of a very serious nature, but when it comes to legislation there are tremendous difficulties.... Several countries have tried it; even England has made a law on the subject but it is not observed.

The children employed in industry are provided by the population of the towns where industry is situated.... If children were not able to work as many hours, it would be necessary to find an additional number of children to send into the various concerns that employ them; for it is quite clear that if a master employs a piecer, and the piecer cannot work the number of hours for which he is engaged at present, another child will have to come and take his place. Now the manufacturing towns have not got this extra supply of children....

Doubtless one *could* state by law that children must not work more than a certain number of hours, but in doing so one would also diminish the number of hours that the master operative can work, and that would do industry an immense amount of harm....

Arch. parl., Chambre des Pairs, 31 May 1839

Billaudel:[2] It is very worrying, gentlemen, to be faced with such serious

---

[1] Hippolyte Philibert Passy (1793-1880) became Minister of Finance in the Soult cabinet on 12 May 1839.

[2] Jean Baptiste Basilide Billaudel (1793-1851) was an experienced engineer and member of several learned academies. In the Chamber he supported the dynastic left.

and difficult problems. On the one hand one thinks in terms of sympathy for human beings who are suffering and unhappy, and of the desire to hurry to their aid with energetic measures; and on the other hand one thinks of liberty of commerce and industry, of respect for parental authority, of respect for misfortune itself, for who would dare to suggest taking away from a father and mother, burdened with a large family, the help they can get from their children's hands?

This is not the place, gentlemen, to examine the pros and cons of economic theory concerning the use of machines in industrial development and free competition between individuals and nations. It cannot be denied that the application of the forces of nature to the making of common objects has been a genuine advance, which has allowed the poverty stricken masses to obtain a host of pleasures previously denied them. We owe this undoubted benefit to the spread of education and the accumulation of capital. But the gathering together in industrial establishments of a large number of people of all ages and both sexes has given rise to disadvantages which were perhaps easy to forsee but are rather difficult to avoid. . . .

Military experts are unanimously of the opinion that people from manufacturing districts are, on the whole, less vigorous than those from the country. . . . In 1837 the number of young men eligible for conscription came to 309,516. 268,631 were rejected because they were not tall enough or because they were unfit. In other words, for every 100 able-bodied soldiers, 86 were rejected. The department of Seine-Inférieure, whose population is largely industrial, had to provide 1,609 men and it rejected 2,044; i.e. for every 100 able-bodied men 126 were rejected, which is half as much again as the general average for France. The town of Rouen, in particular, which was put down to provide 184 men, had to reject 317; i.e for every 100, 166 were eliminated, which is nearly double the national average. Your commission found that at Mulhouse in 1837, gentlemen, the rejects came to 110 per cent; at Elbeuf to 168 per cent; at Nîmes to 147 per cent. Here we have a result beyond question: the manufacturing population is as a rule weak and debilitated. But how far can this sad state of affairs be attributed to the excessive burden of work imposed on children at an early age? This question is tied up with too many factors to be resolved by figures. There is no doubt that such things as town life, the passions aroused among large bodies of people of all ages and both sexes, the example and contagion of vice, excessive debauchery and loose living play a very large part in the gradual deterioration of the constitution, even in the most robust. But one should also note that the factories, in offering easy work which does not demand much physical strength, necessarily appeal to and draw together the least vigorous portions of the population. One might also add that men of this class develop slowly, and the age fixed for the army does not reveal the true physique of the candidates examined. . . .

In the enquiry of 1834, M. Beauvisage, who owes his great success as a manufacturer to hard work and perseverance, stated as follows: 'Our industry may achieve certain brief successes, but morality alone can make them permanent. Our neighbours possess this advantage as a result of the religious faith which still inspires them. In our case only a sound education can teach our workers the good conduct which will ensure their comfort, health, and happiness.' But can one, should one, impose by law the obligation upon parents and manufacturers to keep children who cannot read or write away from the factories? At what age would one allow these children to be taken into the spinning sheds? Is there not a danger that the law would be evaded? Would it not for a certainty be ignored in out-of-the-way factories to the detriment of those in towns? Would you have inspectors to judge between master and man and between father and son? A host of objections spring to mind when one looks at these questions and tries to answer them practically. . . .

Arch. parl., Chambre des Députés, 15 June 1839

2 Lower-class attitudes

(a) *The* Atelier

In 1841 the Chambers passed a law forbidding employment of children under 8 in factories and restricting the number of hours which older children could work (8 to 12 years old, eight daylight hours; 12 to 16 years old, twelve daylight hours). The law did not apply to workshops with fewer than 20 employees, and no adequate provision was made to enforce it. The following criticism comes from a newspaper founded in September 1840 by a group of craftsmen (printers, jewellers, hatters etc.) who took the opportunity to voice their resentment against large-scale industry as well as against the government.

We have said before that the immense progress made by industry in France since the Restoration has been one of the chief causes of the poverty which is undermining the greater part of the population. Everybody knows that agriculture has not followed this upward movement, and that whilst machines have secured inordinate development for industry our agricultural methods have hardly been improved at all. The whole emphasis is upon non-essential or luxury products, whilst those of prime importance are neglected. Country districts are continually supplying large numbers of men to the towns, seduced by the prospect of gain which diminishes rapidly when seen at close quarters. Manufacturers arise by the thousand, whilst fields are either not cultivated at all or are cultivated by backward methods. The shops are full of cheap objects which one might at a pinch do without, whilst absolute necessities are exorbitant. What does it matter to the worker that silk goods are cheap, when bread and meat are dear? He needs food, and he is accustomed to wearing clothes of rough cotton. Let us have the necessaries, and the extras will come later. At the moment we have neither, as the debate on the law concerning child labour has proved. . . .

It has been proved that poor unfortunate children of 5 and 6 years old work 12 to 15 hours a day in unhealthy workshops, at work which is made more terrible by the fact that they are hardly able to move, and growing children need so much exercise. It has been stated that this labour is paid at a rate of 30 to 40 centimes a day, and that it is not the desire for gain which forces parents thus to abuse the authority conferred on them by law, but necessity. Necessity, do you hear, forces them to be executioners! And the most dreadful thing of all is that for years this state of affairs has been getting worse and worse and the government has not bothered – the government which is supposed to see to the security and happiness of all – until statistics and the operation of the call-up proved to it that after half a century of such a régime the French nation would become a nation of cretins and consumptives, unable any longer to produce farmers to feed itself and soldiers to defend itself.

. . . And what has been done, in the end, to stave off disaster? The government has restricted the number of working hours and raised the age at which children can be admitted into factories. What will happen? The millowners will lose nothing, because they will take two children instead of one for the same price, which is only fair. They will adopt the system of 'shifts', as they do in England, and the children on shift work will in the end do more work, better, and consequently less well paid. But the parents whose children were getting 40 centimes and will now get no more than 20, what measures have been taken to compensate them for this decrease in wages? None. . . .

Only when political reform has brought to power men whom we hope will be devoted to the people's interests are we likely to see a beginning made upon the great task of organizing agricultural and industrial production on an altogether different foundation from the present, with association instead of fragmentation, and fraternity and solidarity instead of selfishness.

Atelier, January 1841

(b) *The case of Étienne Robert*

Meanwhile the very poor, who were less articulate, were seldom heard except in the law-courts.

A poor devil called Étienne Robert, of a sickly appearance, with haggard face and eyes dull and sunken, was brought before the correctional police on a charge of vagrancy. He did not attempt to deny the offence with which he was charged, and blamed it on to the fate which had dogged him from birth. 'How can you expect me to be anything but a vagrant?' asked the poor wretch. 'How can you expect me to possess a hearth and shelter for my weary limbs? I was a vagrant before I was born.'

President of the Court: Mind what you are saying. Talk sense.

Accused: I am telling you the truth. I was born on the road, between Angoulême and Périgord. My mother left me there, in a ditch. I was picked up by I don't know who and taken to a hostel, and when I was grown up and had got a trade they wished me good luck and sent me on my way. That's my life story.

President: If you have a trade, why don't you work?

Accused: There isn't always work, and when there is I can't do much. I'm as weak as a kitten. I spend half of my time being ill in hospital, and that doesn't get you a fortune. Look at me now – I've just come out of hospital. I look as though I could do with going back, don't I? But what can I do? They made out that I was all right. So, not having found a job and not having a penny to bless myself with I slept out in Montmartre near a lime-kiln, and they arrested me.

President: What will you do if the Tribunal dismisses you?

Accused: I shall do what I've done all my life – work occasionally, be ill quite a lot, and tramp about most of the time.

President: . . . You take your misfortune very lightly.

Accused: If I get worked up about it, it does no good. I tell you it's fate – the misfortune of my birth is dogging me. I was born on the road and I shall die on the road. A man can't escape his destiny. But don't worry: I shall remain honest. I shall never take anything beyond a share of sunshine and a bed in the fresh air.

The Tribunal, in view of the extenuating circumstances, condemned the fatalistic vagabond to two months imprisonment.

Gazette des Tribunaux, 5 August 1840

3 Middle-class attitudes

(a) *The* Journal des Débats

On 21 November 1831 the silk-workers of Lyon, assisted by detachments of the National Guard, rose in revolt as a result of the refusal of manufacturers to abide by a fixed scale of wages. The following comment, taken from an article by one of the leading liberal publicists of the day, illustrates the growing acceptance of class divisions. The writer advised the disbanding of the Lyon National Guard.

It is no good shutting one's eyes to the facts, for what is the use of pretence and concealment? The revolt of Lyon has brought a great secret into the open: the inherent conflict which exists in society between the haves and the have-nots. Our commercial and industrial society has its plague like all other societies, and this plague consists of the workers. There could be no workshops without workers, and there can be no rest for society with a population of workers always growing and always in want. Diminish commerce, and our society languishes; stop it altogether, and it dies; intensify, develop, and multiply commerce and you multiply at the same time a proletariat which lives from hand to mouth and which the least accident can deprive of the means of subsistence. Ask in any manufacturing town the relative numbers of the industrial and merchant class and of the working class, and you will be frightened at the disproportion. Every manufacturer lives in his factory like the colonial planter in the midst of his slaves, one against a hundred, and the subversion of Lyon is a sort of insurrection of San Domingo.

The trouble is, too, that one cannot avoid the danger by kindness and fair play. You are compassionate, disinterested, content to pay your way; although times are bad you still pay your workers the same wages; why should they be tempted to revolt? Does your fair play keep them from misery? Alas, no! Bread is dear, either because there has been too much rain during the year or too little rain, and the price of bread means that the same sum of money is not enough for the workers. Or perhaps there is a good year and bread is at a reasonable price; but it happens that five hundred miles away, in Russia or Austria or some place where labour is cheap, a factory of your kind has just been set up which sells goods cheaper than you. How are you to put up with the competition? By lowering wages? But then the workers would be abandoned to all the temptations of misery.

Commercial rivalry today has the same effect that the migration of people had of old. Ancient society perished because the people stirred in the deserts of the north and hurled themselves upon each other, until the time came when they invaded the Roman Empire. Today, if corn is cheaper in the Crimea than in England, if cotton can be spun cheaper in Vienna than in Manchester, English society is reduced to dire straits. . . . The barbarians who menace society are not in the Caucasus or in the steppes of Tartary; they are in the suburbs of our industrial cities. . . . Is it surprising that they are tempted to attack the bourgeoisie? They are stronger and more numerous; you have yourselves given them arms; and after all they are suffering horribly from want. . . .

The middle class must recognize clearly what the situation is; it must know exactly where it stands. It has beneath it a proletariat which is agitated and disturbed, without knowing what it wants or where it is going. What does it matter? Things are bad: it must change them. That is the danger that threatens modern society; that is where the barbarians will come from to destroy it. . . .

Members of the middle class, republican or monarchist! Whatever may be the differences of opinion as to the best form of government there can only be one opinion, I imagine, on the need to maintain society. And it is going against the maintenance of society to give political rights and national armaments to those who have nothing to lose and everything to gain.

Saint-Marc Girardin[3] in the *Journal des Débats*
8 December 1831

(b) *Etiquette*

A popular book of etiquette saw fit to instruct genteel persons in proper behaviour towards members of their own class and towards the inferior orders.

If you are caught without umbrella in a shower of rain and someone with an umbrella is going in the same direction, it is proper for you to ask if you can shelter under it. The person applied to should receive the request politely, ask where you are going, and offer to accompany you provided this does not mean them going out of their way and they are

---

[3] Marc (known as Saint-Marc) Girardin (1801–73) played a notable part in left-wing journalism during the last years of the Restoration. In 1830 he was appointed deputy to Guizot in the chair of history at the Sorbonne.

not in a hurry. . . . What I have just said indicates that a person who is really polite will not wait to be asked but will hasten to offer assistance. He or she should make sure that age, sex and appearance present no barrier, however; for sometimes an offer can be received with annoyance or disdain, and for a lady, at least below a certain age, it would be altogether out of place to approach a man. . . . It would be equally out of place to offer assistance to persons from the lower classes, though if such a person asks you, you must agree graciously.

Another rule of behaviour current in the streets concerns asking the way. If you require someone to render you this service you should address them politely and ask in a straightforward manner, 'Madame, or Monsieur, could you tell me the way to so-and-so please?' You must be careful to use this form of address even if the person you approach is a doorkeeper or a fruitseller.

> Mme Celnart, *Manuel complet de la bonne compagnie* (6th ed. Paris, 1833) p. 59

(c) An academic treatise

The following extract is translated from a paper read to the Institute by Charles Dunoyer (1786–1862), a notable economist and left-wing journalist during the Restoration.

Has the government done what it could and should for the labouring classes? . . . On this subject I shall confine myself to the few observations which follow.

First: society taken as a whole has no rights over the property of its members taken as individuals. It is impossible to see what claim it *could* have to riches which are not of its own making, and, since it has not made them, on what ground it dare deny them to those who have created them. In the second place: if society is not master of the property of those who possess something, it is under no obligation to those who possess nothing. Society, like the individual, only owes the equivalent of what it has received; and when the needy classes scarcely pay enough to be protected it is impossible to see what right they have to make demands about being raised up and succoured.

Some people say that the condition of these people is the *fault* of society, and that reparation should be made to them. But how can they prove it? There can be no doubt that many evils have been committed in the world at all times, in all professions and in all classes, and that nothing could be more desirable, for the present and the future, than to see the disappearance of all injustice in the relationship between men and their means of enrichment; but who dare think of turning the clock back? What power would be capable of discerning the good and bad ingredients in each individual fortune, of making a just settlement of the affairs of society and of saying to each family, 'That, exactly, out of the mass of riches that labour has created upon our soil during fourteen centuries, is the part that should revert to you'? Would it not be the last degree of stupidity and madness to attempt such a settlement? Do you think, moreover, that it would be possible to bring it to a successful conclusion and that it would result in a distribution of wealth very different from what we have at present? Are there not good reasons for believing that the families of the poor ought to impute a large part of their misfortunes to themselves or their begettors? Is there any difficulty in pointing out thousands of men, who, by their idleness and licentiousness and above all by the criminal abuse they make of their reproductive powers, behave as if on purpose to aggravate their own misfortune and extend their misery over a still larger area? Do you think society owes any reparation to people who are the saddest and heaviest of its burdens?

Those who say, moreover, that society owes work, bread and instruction to the needy speak too easily. Do they think that it would be an easy thing to offer people work – fruitful and productive work? Is it the function of society to create industrial enterprises and invent productive work for those who don't know how to find it? Is such a thing within its power? Society owes everybody justice and protection: it owes nobody lucrative employment, education or bread in default of work. Society, taken as a whole, has no funds of its own; it can only give to one lot of people by taking away from another, and when it wants to meddle and distribute the general wealth other than in the way it is distributed by nature it nearly always does harm. It denudes the good plants for the sake of the weeds. It despoils healthy families, which need help from no-one, to uphold feeble or vicious families which are far from being equally worthy of its interest.

Ch. Dunoyer, Mémoire à consulter sur quelques-
unes des principales questions que la Révolution de
Juillet a fait naître (Paris, 1835) pp. 128, 132-5

4   Fictional attitudes

In the 1840s, a sentimental humanitarianism became fashionable among the middle classes. Writers of serial stories for the newspapers described the life of the down-and-out in highly coloured terms, designed to give the impression that the poor were all good at heart and could not be blamed for viciousness bred by circumstances. The following extract is taken from one of the most popular of the serial stories, published in 1841 by the *Journal des Débats*. The hero, a wealthy young man called Rudolph, is sitting in a squalid inn in a disreputable district of Paris talking to one of the habitués, an ex-convict nicknamed the *Chourineur* (literally, one who murders by knifing his victim).

The Slasher emptied his glass and began thus:

'I can't remember having slept in what you might call a bed until I was nineteen (a ripe old age) when I joined the army. . . . The stones of the Louvre, the lime-kilns of Clichy and the quarries of Montrouge – those were the hôtels of my youth. So, you see, I actually had a house in Paris and one in the country.'

'And what was your trade?'

'Faith, master, I have a dim recollection of having wandered about in my childhood with an old rag-picker who used to knock me about unmercifully. . . . My first job was helping the knackers to cut the horses' throats at Montfauçon. I was ten or twelve years old. When I first started to slash the poor old beasts it had quite an effect on me, but after a month or so I thought nothing of it. On the contrary, I began to like the job. Nobody else had a knife as sharp and pointed as mine, and that gave me the urge to use it. When I had slaughtered my animals I would be given a piece off the rump of some horse that had died of disease. . . and then I was as happy as a king! I went with it into my lime-kiln like a wolf into his lair, and there, with the permission of the lime-burners, I made a marvellous fry on the ashes. . . . My birthplace? The first corner of any road you come to, either on the left or the right going up or coming down the kennel.'

'Have you cursed your father and mother for abandoning you?'

'A fat lot of good that would have done me! But it's true they played me a scurvy trick in bringing me into the world. I wouldn't have minded if they had made me like the good Lord ought to have made beggars – unable to feel cold, hunger or thirst. It wouldn't have cost him anything, and it wouldn't have cost beggars so much to stay honest.'

'You were frozen and hungry, and you did not steal? . . . Were you afraid of going to gaol?'

'Heck, no!' said the Slasher, shrugging his shoulders and roaring with laughter. 'Whilst I was honest I was famished: if I had turned thief they would have fed me in prison! I didn't steal because – because – why, simply because it never entered my head to steal.'

This truly noble speech, the significance of which was not understood by the Slasher, greatly astonished Rudolph. He felt that the poor man who had remained honest in the midst of the most cruel privations was doubly worthy, since the punishment of the crime could have assured him of assistance. Rudolph held out his hand to this luckless savage of civilisation, whom misery had never wholly corrupted. The Slasher looked at his host with astonishment – almost with respect. He hardly dared to touch the hand that was offered to him, for he had a feeling that there was a wide abyss between him and Rudolph. . . .

Rudolph continued coolly, not wishing him to detect the emotion he felt, 'Did you remain a knacker's assistant for long?'

'I should think I did! By the time I was about sixteen and my voice had broken, it had become a raging passion with me to cut and slash. I gave up food and drink for it; I thought of nothing else. You should have seen me in the thick of my work! Except for an old pair of cotton trousers I was quite naked. When I had my well-sharpened knife in my hand and as many as fifteen or twenty horses lined up around me waiting their turn (no kidding!) – by Jove! when I began to slaughter them I don't know what got into me. I was like a fury! My ears buzzed! I saw red – everything was red! And I slashed, and slashed, and slashed, until the knife fell from my hands. God! what happiness! I couldn't have been happier if I'd been a millionaire.'

'And that was what gave you the habit of slashing,' said Rudolph.

'Could have been. But when I was turned sixteen the mania became so strong that once I began slashing I went mad, and I spoilt my work. Yes, I damaged the hides by slashing them to ribbons. In the end they turned me out of the yard. . . . I sought my bread elsewhere and didn't find it easily; my belly was often empty in those days. At last I got work in the quarries at Montrouge, but at the end of two years I was fed up with being like a squirrel in a cage, quarrying stone for 20 sous a day. I was tall and strong, so I joined the army. . . .'

'With your strength and courage, and your mania for slashing, you would probably have been made an officer if there had been a war.'

'My God, your telling me! Slashing at the English and Prussians would have suited me even better than slashing at old horses. But there was no war, worse luck; only drilling. . . . One day the sergeant hustled me to make me get a move on (quite right, as I was straggling). That annoyed me, so I balked. He pushed me, so I pushed him; he collared me, and I punched him on the head. They fell on me, and then my blood was really up and I saw red. I had a knife in my hand (I belonged to the cook-house) and I went at it – slashing and slashing as if I was in the slaughter house. I killed the sergeant and wounded two soldiers – it was a real shambles. The three of them got eleven wounds – yes, eleven! There was blood everywhere – blood – like being in a charnel house –'

The brigand dropped his head with a dull, haggard look, and remained silent for a moment.

'What are you thinking about, Slasher?' asked Rudolph, observing him with interest.

'Nothing, nothing,' he said brusquely, then continued with the same devil-may-care attitude, 'At last they got a grip on me and took me before the Beak, and I was booked for the high-jump.'

'Were you rescued, then?'

'No. I was given fifteen years in the galleys instead of being scragged. I forgot to tell you – whilst I was in the army I fished out two comrades who were drowning in the Marne (we were in barracks at Melun). Another time, . . . when we were in barracks at Rouen, all the wooden houses (proper hovels they were) in one quarter caught fire and blazed like matchwood. I was part of the fire squad, and when we got there they yelled to me that there was an old woman trapped in her bedroom by the flames. I ran to the place, and my hat! how it burned! It reminded me of my lime-kiln in the good old days. However, I saved the old woman. . . . My barrister was so wily that he got my sentence commuted, and instead of the scaffold I was sent to the hulks for fifteen years. When I first realized that I was not going to be put to death I could have wrung the prating fool's neck. Do you understand, master?

'You were sorry to have your sentence commuted?'

'Yes. Those who sport with the knife should be shaved by Jack Ketch; and for those who steal, the irons. To every man his deserts. But to force a man to go on living when he has committed murder! I tell you, the Beaks don't know what it does to you in the early days.'

'Did you feel remorse, then, Slasher?'

'Remorse? No, not since I served my time,' said the Savage. 'But before that, never a night passed but what I saw, like a nightmare, the sergeant and soldiers whom I had slaughtered. That is, they were not alone,' added the brigand, in something like terror, 'they were in tens, and dozens, and hundreds, waiting their turn in a kind of slaughterhouse, like the horses that I slaughtered at Montfauçon waited their turn. Then I saw red and began to slash and slash at those men, like I used to do at the horses. But the more soldiers I hacked down the more appeared. And as they died they gave me such a gentle look – such a gentle look – that I cursed myself for killing them, but I couldn't stop myself. And that wasn't all. I never had a brother, yet it seemed as if every one of these men I killed was my brother, and I would have died for them. .... At last, when I could bear it no longer, I used to wake up bathed in sweat as cold as melting snow.'

... 'What did you do when you came out, Slasher?'

'I offered myself to the master bargeman of the Quai St. Paul, and I get my living there.'

'But since in spite of all you were never a thief, why do you live in the Cité?,'

'Where would you have me live? Who likes to be seen with an ex-convict? Besides, I should be bored on my own; I like society, and here I am with my own kind.'

'How much do you get a day?'

'Thirty-five sous. That'll last whilst I have strength; and then I shall take a rake and wicker-basket like the old rag-picker I see in the recollections of my childhood.'

'And after all that, you are not unhappy.'

'There are plenty worse off than me. Without the dreams of the murdered sergeant and soldiers that I sometimes still get I could die happily like anyone else at the side of the road or in the workhouse. But the dream – God! I don't even like to think of it,' said the Slasher, and he knocked the ash from his pipe on the corner of the table.

Eugene Sue, *Les Mystères de Paris*, ch. IV

5   The Organization of Labour

Theories concerning social reorganization abounded in the late 'thirties and 'forties. Among the best known, at least among the upper ranks of the working class such as skilled workmen in the Paris luxury trades, was Louis Blanc's *Organization of Labour* (1839). Louis Blanc (1811-82) was a journalist by profession. His views were distinguished from those of more utopian socialists such as Proudhon and Cabet by his acceptance of the class struggle and by his insistence that the workers must receive state aid in the early stages of their campaign against capitalism. Louis Blanc was taken into the government when the Second Republic was proclaimed in February 1848, but he was not allowed to give full rein to his ideas, and the famous National Workshops organised by Émile Thomas were a mere travesty of the social workshops which Louis Blanc had advocated.

When he had only a few days left to live, Louis XI was suddenly seized with a tremendous fear. His courtiers dared not utter in his hearing the dreadful word, the inevitable word, death. He himself tried miserably to make his dull gaze shine with the light of an unreal joy, as though he could stave off death by denying its approach. He hid his pallor. He tried hard not to totter when he walked. He said to his doctor, 'Just look at me! I was never better.'

Society is doing the same thing today. It feels itself to be dying yet denies its decay. It surrounds itself with all the delusions of wealth and all the vain pomp of a power which is vanishing, and puffs itself up in the very crisis of its difficulties. The privileged ranks of modern society resemble that child of Sparta who smiled whilst hiding within his robe the fox that gnawed at his entrails. They too display a smiling face: they make every effort to be gay. But anxiety dwells in their hearts and preys upon them. The ghost of revolutions is at all their feasts.

. . . I ask you, who is really interested in maintaining the social order, such as it is today? No-one; no-one at all. I myself am quite convinced that the unhappiness created by an imperfect civilization spreads, in different forms, over the whole of society. Take the life of the rich – it is full of bitterness. Why? Is it because they lack health, youth or flatterers? Is it because they think they have no friends? It is because they have exhausted all pleasure – that is their misery. They have drained desire – that is their disease. . . . The bourgeoisie established its domination through that tyrannical principle, unbridled competition; but behold, it is through unbridled competition that we see the bourgeoisie perishing today. 'I have two millions,' you say, 'and my rival only has one. I shall undercut him in the market and ruin him for a certainty.' Stupid and senseless man! Do you not see that tomorrow some ruthless Rothschild, using your very own weapons, will destroy you?

. . . As for the poor man, is he a member of society or is he its enemy? Let me tell you.

He sees all around him the soil occupied. Can he sow seed on his own account? No, because the right of first occupant has become the right of ownership. Can he pick the fruit that the hand of God has caused to ripen along man's path? No, because the fruits have been 'appropriated' like the soil. Can he take to hunting or fishing? No, because they are a right affirmed by the government. Can he draw water from a fountain in the middle of a field? No, because the owner of the field by virtue of the right of access is owner of the fountain. Can he, when he is overcome with fatigue and has no shelter, sleep on the pavement in the streets? No, because there are laws against vagrancy. Can he flee from this homicidal fatherland where everything is denied him, and go seek a means of livelihood far from the place which gave him birth?

No, because he can only change his country on certain conditions which are impossible for him to fulfil. What will the poor man do, then? He will say to you, 'I have hands, brains, strength, youth. Take them all, and in exchange give me a little bread.' That is what the proletariat does and says today. But at this point you can reply to the poor man, 'I have no work to give you.' What would you have him do then?

The outcome of all this is very simple. *Guarantee* work for the poor. You will still have done very little in the cause of justice, and you will still be a long way from the reign of fraternity, but at least you will have warded off the worst perils and allayed revolt. Have you thought of that? When a man who asks to live by serving society is fatally reduced to attacking it under pain of death, his apparent aggression is really justifiable self-defence, and the society which strikes him is not his judge but his assassin.

The question, therefore, is this. Can competition *guarantee* work for the poor? Put in that way, the answer is obvious. What is competition, as far as the worker is concerned? It is work put up for auction. An employer needs a worker: three come along. 'How much do you want for your labour?' Three francs – I have a wife and children. 'O.K. And you?' Two and a half francs – I have no children, but I have a wife. 'Good show. What about you?' Two francs will do for me – I am on my own. 'Right, the job's yours.'. . .

Conclusion: how one could, in our opinion, organize labour. The government should be considered the supreme regulator of production, and should be invested with large powers in order to accomplish its task. This task should consist of making use of the weapon of competition in order to get rid of competition.

The government should raise a loan, and use the proceeds to create social workshops in the most important branches of the nation's industry. Since these creations could involve considerable outlay of money, the number of workshops created to start with should be strictly limited, but by virtue of their very organization they would be endowed with immense powers of expansion, as we shall see later.

The government being the sole founder of the social workshops, it should be the government which draws up the rules for them. These rules, debated and passed by the nation's representatives, should have the form and force of law.

Work in the social workshops would be offered to all workers presenting guarantees of good behaviour, to a number not exceeding the capital originally invested for the purchase of tools. Although the false and anti-social education given to the present generation makes it difficult to seek incentives elsewhere than in extra pay, wages should be equal, and new educational methods must be introduced to change people's ideas and outlook. For the first year following the establishment of the social workshops the government would regulate the hierarchy of employment, but after the first year it would no longer be the same. The workers would have had time to get to know each other, and since all would be equally concerned in the success of the association, as we shall see, the hierarchy would rest on an elective basis.

Every year an account should be taken of the net profit, and it should be divided into three parts. One part should be distributed in equal portions among members of the association. The second should be assigned to the support of the aged, sick and infirm, and to the alleviation of crises falling upon other industries, since all industries would owe each other succour and support. The third and last should be allotted to providing tools for those who wish to join the association, in such a manner that it would be able to expand indefinitely. . . .

Once a social workshop had been launched according to these principles, one can readily see what the results would be. In every main industry the machine industry, for instance, or the silk or cotton industry, or the printing industry – there would be a social workshop competing with private industry. Would the struggle last long? No, because the social workshop would have over the private workshop the advantage which results from communal life being cheaper, and from a mode of organization in which all the workers without exception are interested in producing quickly and well.

Louis Blanc, *L'Organisation du travail* (5th ed., Paris, 1848)

6   The Voyage to Icaria

More popular among the miscellaneous working class of French cities was the work of Étienne Cabet (1788-1856), whose *Voyage en Icarie*, first published in 1840, had run into five editions by 1848. Some estimates give Cabet as many as 200,000 disciples by the time the revolution broke out. The *Voyage* took the form of a novel in which an English 'milord', hearing of a classless community called Icaria where all property was held in common, determined to visit it. He was greeted with typical kindness by the Icarians, who admitted him to membership of a family and made arrangements for an extensive tour of inspection, punctuated by long lectures. Through this unpromising medium, Cabet's simplicity and sincerity shine to this day.

I knew that Icar[4] had arranged for the master-plan of a house to be drawn up, after he had consulted the Housing Committee and the whole People and had ordered houses in other countries to be inspected;[5] so I was expecting to see a house perfect in every respect, above all in matters of comfort and cleanliness. Even so, my expectations were surpassed. ... It combines everything imaginable in the way of necessity and usefulness, and one might even say of charm.

Each house has three floors, not counting the ground floor, with three, four, or five windows to each floor. Below the ground floor are the cellars and storage places for wood and coal, the floors being some five or six feet below the pavement and the roofs three or four feet above. The lady of the house explained how the wood, coal, etc. are conveyed from the vehicle into these underground areas by machine, without touching and dirtying the pavement. Afterwards she showed us how the things are brought up in baskets or bins to the kitchen or upper floors by means of openings in the ceiling and little machines which make the use of personal labour unnecessary. On the ground floor there are no stores or porters' lodges, but. . . a dining room, a kitchen and all its appurtenances, a little parlour serving as a study, a little work-room for men and another for women containing all the equipment one generally has need of in a household, a little poultry yard, a shed for garden tools, and the garden behind. The first floor consists of a large drawing room containing musical instruments. The other rooms and all those on the other floors are bedrooms or rooms for other purposes. All the windows open outwards and are provided with balconies. Everything is done to make the staircases wide and elegant without taking up too much room.

'What a view!' I cried when we reached the terrace, which is at the top of the house surrounded by a balustrade and covered with flowers, forming another garden with a view which is something quite magnificent.

'On fine summer evenings,' said the lady of the house, 'nearly all the families join each other on their terraces to take the air, playing and singing and eating supper. You will see! It is quite charming.'

Eugène and I also admired the chimneys and the system of heating which spread equal warmth everywhere with the greatest economy and without the fear of horrid smoke or of fires breaking out.

[4] Icar was the benevolent despot who presided over the setting up of the community in the first instance.

[5] Public affairs in Cabet's community were regulated by the direct intervention of the whole people. (Direct democracy – the ideal of the Parisian sans-culottes in the French Revolution.)

'Just see how the doors and windows move on their hinges without any noise, as though they were shutting by themselves!' said Eugène, 'and how perfectly they keep the cold air out!'

'Yet see at the same time how all our rooms are well ventilated,' said the mistress, 'without opening doors or windows, by means of these vents through to the outside, which open and shut automatically.'

But it was above all the whole system devised for cleanliness which I admired most enthusiastically, along with the system designed to save the women all laborious and distasteful jobs in the house. There is not a thing that has not been done to ensure cleanliness. The lower parts, which are the most likely to get dirty, are covered with glazed tiles or with a kind of paint which is dirt resistant and can easily be washed. Drinking water and washing water, brought from high reservoirs and carried up as far as the terrace, is distributed to all floors and even to each room by means of pipes and taps, whilst dirty water and all impurities are carried away, without standing at all and without spreading any bad smells, by large underground pipes in the roads. All the places which are naturally the most disgusting are those where art has made the greatest efforts to dispel all traces of unpleasantness, and one of the prettiest statues commissioned by the Republic is that which one sees in all houses, above the door of a charming little closet, immortalising the name of a woman who invented a device for getting rid of foul smells.

As for the housework, which is done not by servants but by the women and children in each family, I could not sufficiently admire the care the Republic has taken to free domestic work from all fatiguing and distasteful aspects.

'Cleaning is almost nothing,' said the mother of the family, 'and the other jobs are even less onerous. Not only does education and public opinion condition us women to doing these jobs without resentment and annoyance, but they make these jobs pleasing and dear to us by reminding us all the time that this is the only means of enjoying an inestimable advantage – that of not having paid outsiders to serve us and our families. Moreover, thanks to our good Icar and our beloved Republic,[6] all man's imagination works incessantly to make us happy and to simplify our domestic duties. The two principal meals, lunch and dinner, are taken out,[7] and are prepared by the national cooks; whilst all our clothing, both men's and women's, and all our linen is supplied by

[6] Cabet explained in the Preface that the term 'republic' was used to describe a community governed in the interests of the whole people, regardless of the type of government. A constitutional monarch was not precluded.

[7] An earlier chapter describes these sumptuous repasts, served in a magnificent hall decorated with flowers and with orchestras playing.

the Republic's workshops, so that we are only responsible for upkeep, repairs, and the two simplest meals which need only the most pleasant preparations in the kitchen. Talking of our kitchen, come back and have a look at it! See the cooker, the stove, the taps for hot and cold water, all the little gadgets and utensils – can you possibly imagine anything neater and more convenient? Was he not the most gallant as well as the most ingenious of architects who devised everything to make us love our work? All the girls like to sing charming songs in honour of the young and gallant architect of the kitchens.'

Such is a house in Icaria. All the houses in the towns are the same on the inside, and each is occupied by a single family. . . . When a family gets larger (as frequently happens), it occupies two houses adjacent to each other with a communicating door on the inside. Since all the houses are identical, the people next door usually leave their house voluntarily to take another, or the magistrate obliges them to do so if they refuse. . . . In such cases, furniture as well as houses being absolutely the same, each family takes only a few personal things and leaves its house fully furnished to take another fully furnished.

E. Cabet, *Voyage en Icarie* (5th ed., Paris 1848) ch. IX

XIV

THE DOWNFALL OF THE RÉGIME

1 The banquet campaign

In the summer of 1847, opposition deputies sponsored a series of banquets to obtain support for their campaign to extend the franchise. At the banquets, which were a device for circumventing the ban on public meetings, subscribers sat down to a meal of cold meat, then listened to speeches and drank toasts. Sometimes spectators were admitted for a smaller fee. About 80 banquets were held up and down the country. It was soon discovered that their character varied according to whether moderate or radical deputies had been invited, and the original sponsors were only too ready to drop the idea after reading reports of speeches like the following, made by Ledru-Rollin[1] at Lille on 9 September 1847.

Fellow citizens: To the workers! To their imprescriptible rights and sacred interests, hitherto unrecognized! Their rights? After two revolutions they have conquered their rights, and no-one today could deny them in principle, but in practice they are deferred indefinitely. (True, true!). We are asked what rights we want to confer on the people. They are incapable – ignorant. The people? The term means anarchy, revolution, bloodshed. (Lengthy disturbance.)

Gentlemen, you in this industrial town know the people well. (Yes, and we love them!) Do you believe that this picture is true? (No, no!) Oh, no doubt if we consult the hack writers we shall find that the people *are* like that. (Bravo! bravo!) No doubt, too, if we glance through the pages of the fashionable novelists we shall find that the people are like that. But where do they get their evidence? From Paris – from the part of the city that furnishes the habitual criminals. Seeking amongst the fantastic and the hideous for dramatic effect, they arrive

[1] Alexandre Auguste Ledru-Rollin (1807-74) had made his name as counsel for the defence in the political trials of 1834-5. In 1841 he was elected to the Chamber, where he sat on the extreme left. In 1843 he founded a newspaper, the *Réforme*, which published articles by Louis Blanc.

by an astonishing stretch of the imagination at the conclusion that the degraded and hideous men who haunt these dens are the people. Oh, gentlemen! those are not the people. It is not in those places that you will see them. (No, no!) You have to betake yourself to one of these manufacturing towns where the masters, hard-pressed themselves by fierce rivalry from the capital (true!), can no longer break even because all the markets are closed to them and our flag is crushed underfoot. (Sensation.) These masters, I say, are obliged to lower wages. It is not they who are to blame: it is the government. (Hear, hear!) It is the government which doesn't allow them to find markets for their industry. In these towns it is the people who suffer. For what happens? Very often they see their daughters obliged to turn to prostitution to make up their wages. (Lively sensation.) They see their children crying, and the father has no food to give them. (Prolonged disturbance.) Yet, gentlemen, these men suffer in silence, and if sickness and debility does not incapacitate them, when the time comes to defend their country it is they who are there. (Hear, hear!) That is what the people of the towns are like. (Well said!) . . .

You will agree that any form of government that does not conform to the principle that the people have a right to be represented is bad. I say that anyone who contributes his blood, his toil or his money has a right to take part in the government that disposes of his riches. . . . I understand the different degrees that operate in matters of reform – the cautious opinions, the nervous people. (Ironical laughter.) I tolerate their view, but it isn't mine! (Jolly good!) They say there is corruption everywhere, yet they propose modest terms that can do no good. . . . Allow me to make a comparison. You know that in Egypt, in the Delta where there are pools of water, pestilence and corruption set in; then the flood comes and the waves roll over everything, and lo and behold it sweeps away all the impurities, the pestilence disappears, and everywhere around becomes fertile and one sees nothing but abundance and purity. (Prolonged agitation.) That is why, gentlemen, I want universal suffrage!

Report taken from the *Messager du Nord*, 10
September 1847: *Arch. nat.* BB^{30}296

2   Public scandals

Early in 1847 the public was informed that a former Minister of Public Works, Teste, had received a bribe of 94,000 francs from a former Minister for War,

Cubières, who wished to obtain concessions in a salt mine. Before the trial came on, Émile Girardin in the *Presse* 'revealed' other shady transactions by government officials, such as the sale of theatre patents, crosses of the Legion of Honour, and even peerages. His allegations were discussed in both Chambers and dismissed for lack of evidence. Later (July), the trial of Teste and Cubières resulted in their condemnation and an attempt at suicide by Teste. This was followed (24 August) by one of the ghastliest crimes of the century, in which the Duc de Choiseul-Praslin murdered his wife, the daughter of General Sébastiani, who had borne him eleven children. The duke committed suicide after his arrest, in circumstances which looked like connivance on the part of the authorities. These and other scandals created the impression of a general rottenness amongst the ruling élite. The public prosecutor at Colmar commented on the situation to the Minister of Justice in the following letter, dated 9 September 1847.

Dear Sir,
    I have the honour of sending you my report on the state of justice and morals within my area. . . .
    The people of Alsace are essentially lovers of order. That is why, in spite of a leaning towards opposition (a leaning which explains the success of some eccentric local newspapers) they invariably since 1830 sent conservative deputies to the Chamber. They read everywhere that the government was corrupt, but they did not see any corruption so they did not believe in it. When, however, a single case was brought into the limelight and confirmed in the law courts, it gave credence to all the previous accusations; and when further incidents followed, people ended by persuading themselves in all good faith that the authorities were not pure – that they were accomplices in all the dishonest transactions that were being revealed one after the other, if only by turning a blind eye upon them. Jumping in this way from the particular to the general, they failed to see that any vast administration is likely to contain a few deplorable delinquents, but that no government has ever been more ready to punish them and more inflexible in its respect for equality before the law. However unreasonable this attitude may be, it is nonetheless real. . . .
    This attitude, my dear Sir, will explain to you the reform banquets at Colmar and Strasbourg. It will explain above all the presence at these banquets of a large number of conservatives. They seem to have wanted to make a protest against immorality, which they believe to be more widespread than it really is, and thereby to disclaim responsibility for a situation which appears to them to affect the whole of the conservative party. That is also how it has come about that the General Council of Haut-Rhin has for the first time declared in favour of elec-

toral and parliamentary reform. The opposition, which knows how to take advantage of every circumstance, is exploiting these developments and talking loudly about these so-called converts, whom it will lose in no time. The favourite theme, harped on from all angles, is the supposed corruption of the whole of society; but it will not stand the test of time, and the moment is not far off when this stupid bogey will disappear before the light of truth. . . .

Arch. nat. BB^{18}1414

3   Official complacency

(a) *The king's speech*

The king's speech to the Chambers at the opening of the parliamentary session expressed the government view that, having survived the economic crisis of 1845-7, there was little to be feared. Agitation was described as the work of an ill-disposed minority.

I am happy, in coming among you once more, that I no longer have to bewail the suffering that food shortage brought upon our country. France has borne it with a courage that I cannot contemplate without deep emotion. Never in such circumstances have law and order and freedom of commerce been so generally maintained. The unfailing zeal of private charity has seconded our public efforts. Our trade, thanks to wise management, has been only slightly affected by the crisis, which has been felt also in other countries. We are coming to the end of our trials. Heaven has blessed the work of men, and abundant harvests are restoring well-being and security everywhere. . . .

Gentlemen, the older I get the more wholeheartedly I devote to the service of France, and to the care of her interests, dignity and happiness, all that God has given me and preserves to me in the way of energy and strength. In the midst of the agitation which blind or hostile passions are fomenting, one conviction inspires and upholds me: it is that we possess in constitutional monarchy . . . the sure means of surmounting all these obstacles and of satisfying all the material and moral interests of our dear country. Let us maintain firmly, in accordance with the Charter, the social order and all its conditions. Let us guarantee faithfully, in accordance with the Charter, public liberty and all its developments. We shall then transmit intact, to the generations which come after us, the trust that has been confided in us, and they will bless us for having founded and defended the edifice in whose shelter they live, happy and free.

Annales du Parlement Français: Séance royale du 28 décembre 1847

(b) *The* Journal des chemins de fer

Many well-informed persons shared the government's complacency, as can be seen in the following review of the economic situation, published in a leading business journal.

The year 1847 opened under the most gloomy auspices, with anxiety concerning the Bank of France, whose holdings were diminishing rapidly on account of the export of currency due to the food shortage. To try and stop the withdrawal of currency the Bank decided to raise its rate of discount from 4 per cent to 5 per cent as from 14 January, and to borrow bullion to the time of 40 million from the Bank of England. The Paris market had not yet recovered from the fears aroused by this news when the rate on Treasury bonds was raised to 5 per cent. . . . It was concluded from this measure that the Treasury had need of money and could no longer obtain it at a lower rate of interest. In vain did M. Lacave-Laplange, the Finance Minister, make a reassuring speech in the Chamber in which he insisted that the financial situation gave no cause for alarm and no reason to think that there would be need for another loan. No-one could believe him, and people were sorry to see that instead of presenting himself at once on the European market to negotiate a loan which very quickly became indispensable he preferred to hide the needs of the Treasury and put things off, at the risk of being forstalled by other powers who were equally in need of raising loans. In fact, towards the end of February, the British government announced a loan of 8 million sterling at 3 per cent and negotiated it 8 days later at 89½. Government and railway stock continued to fall in both London and Paris after the negotiation of this loan. Enormous sums in gold and silver were continually exported from France and England to Russia and the United States as a result of speculation in grain. . . .

The crisis was nothing like as serious in France as it was in Great Britain. Let it be said first and foremost that the Paris bourse remained steady to the last, and we did not suffer the failure of a single one of our banking houses. . . .

The railways were seriously affected by all the ups and downs in the French funds. . . . Discouragement was such in the early months of the year that everybody demanded that the Chambers take steps to stave off complete ruin. . . . It was not until the end of May, after the replacement of M. Dumon by M. Jayr[2] that the latter presented two bills to modify the statutes of the Paris-Lyon and Lyon-Avignon lines. These bills, like those presented at the beginning of June for the Montereau, Dieppe and Versailles lines, were badly received by the shareholders. They had hoped to obtain a guaranteed interest, but this clause had been rejected for all the lines concerned. . . . Speculation several times dominated shares in the Marseilles line, which underwent enormous and frequent fluctuations. . . . The year 1847 was more unfavourable for shares in the Havre line than for any other in operation. They went down and down and settled at the lowest price of the year. There were complaints that the returns did not justify the hopes to which this line had given rise. . . . Shares in the Bordeaux line fell rapidly below par. . . . Business was considerable throughout the year in the shares of the Nord line, and the probable yield of this line gave rise to lively controversy not only in the papers but even more among groups of speculators. The monetary crisis threw a large proportion of the shares on to the market. English capitalists, especially, who possessed a lot of them, sold them, and also their shares in the Rouen, Havre and Orleans lines. . . . Two railway companies reached the point of liquidation, at the risk of having their deposits confiscated by the government: those of the Lyon-Avignon and Bordeaux-Cette lines.

We can say nothing as yet of the year that is just opening, except that it cannot possibly reproduce the unfortunate circumstances which dogged last year. One cannot deny that the situation now seems very favourable. The food crisis no longer exists, and the monetary crisis which resulted from it has given way, in England and France, to a comparative abundance of currency. . . . As for the political questions which so deeply affected public credit, they have lost much of their importance. We must hope, therefore, never to see again the low levels reached in September 1847, which will remain an exception in the annals of the railway companies.

Journal des chemins de fer, 1 January 1848

4   De Tocqueville's warning

One of the few people who did not share the Establishment's complacency was Count Alexis de Tocqueville (1805-59), the great expert in political institutions, who issued a dramatic warning to his fellow deputies during the debate on the

[2] As Minister for Public Works.

king's speech. His friends thought he was being alarmist, and he admitted afterwards that he was surprised when his prophesy was so soon fulfilled.

Gentlemen, I may be wrong, but it seems to me that the present state of affairs, the present state of opinion, the state of feeling in France is of a kind to alarm and distress one. For my own part I can honestly say in this Chamber that for the first time in fifteen years I feel a certain fear for the future; and what makes me think that I am not altogether wrong is that I am not alone in my impression. I believe I can call on all my hearers and that they will all say that in the constituencies they represent there is the same impression – that a certain malaise, a certain fear has taken hold of men's minds; that for the first time in perhaps sixteen years the feeling, the instinct of instability – that feeling which is the precursor of revolutions, which often announces them and has sometimes given birth to them – that this feeling exists to a very serious degree in the country.

... The cabinet itself admits to some extent the truth of the impression to which I refer, but it attributes it to certain particular causes, certain recent accidents of public life; to the banquets which have caused agitation, to speeches which have excited passion.

Gentlemen, I am afraid that to attribute the kind of malaise I am speaking of to the causes I have just mentioned is to take the symptoms for the disease. I myself am convinced that the disease is not there; it is more general and more deep-seated. This disease, which believe me must be cured at all costs, for I tell you it will carry us all off if we are not careful, is the spirit of the times, the attitude of the public. ...

If I take a close look at the governing class, the class with rights, and at the class which is governed, what is taking place frightens and disturbs me. To speak first of what I have called the governing class (and note that I include in this class not only what is wrongly called in our day the middle class, but all those who, whatever their position, enjoy rights in the most general sense of the word), I say that what goes on within this class disturbs and frightens me. I can express what I see there in a word, gentlemen: the public attitude is changing, has already changed profoundly, and is changing more and more every day. More and more, public spirit and sentiment is being replaced by self-interest, private ambition, and attitudes borrowed from private life and private interests.

It is not my intention, gentlemen, to force the Chamber to dwell too much on these unpleasant facts. I confine myself to addressing my adversaries, my colleagues of the ministerial majority. I ask them to

make for themselves a sort of statistical review of the electoral colleges
which have sent them to this Chamber, putting in the first category all
those who vote for them not on account of political opinion but for
reasons of personal friendship and neighbourliness. In a second category, let them put all those who vote for them not out of any public or
general interest but out of purely local interest. To this second category
let them add a third, composed of those who vote for them entirely
from motives of personal interest, and I ask them if those who vote out
of disinterested public spirit and as a result of opinion and public
feeling form the majority. I am sure they will easily discover the reverse.
I shall presume to ask them, further, if to their knowledge, in the last 5,
10, 15 years, the number of those voting for them out of personal and
private interest has not grown continually greater, while the number of
those voting out of political opinion has decreased. I shall ask them
finally if they do not see around them, taking root little by little in the
opinion of the public, a sort of strange tolerance for the facts I am
speaking of; if there is not developing little by little a sort of vulgar and
mean attitude, according to which a man who qualifies for certain
political rights owes it to himself, to his children, his wife and his parents
to make personal usage of those rights in the interests of all; if this is not
growing gradually until it is becoming a kind of duty on the part of
the father of a family? . . .

France was the first to give to the world, amid the thunderous
tumult of her first revolution, principles which have since been found
to be regenerative principles for all human societies. That was her
glory; that was the most precious thing about her. Well, gentlemen, it
is those principles that our example is weakening today. The application that we seem to be making of them ourselves is causing the world
to doubt. Europe, which is watching us, is beginning to wonder
whether we were right or wrong; she is wondering whether we are
indeed leading human society towards a happier and more prosperous
future, as we have so often said, or whether we are dragging it in our
wake towards moral degradation and ruin. . . .

Gentlemen, if the spectacle we are producing has such an effect when
seen from afar, from the confines of Europe, what effect do you think
it is having in France itself, upon the classes which have no rights and
are watching us, from out of the idleness to which our laws condemn
them, acting alone in this great theatre? What do you think is the effect
produced on them by such a spectacle? For my part I am alarmed.
People say there is no danger because there is no uprising; that because
there is no obvious disorder on the surface of society, revolution is a

long way off. Gentlemen, let me tell you in all sincerity that I believe you to be mistaken. It is true that there is no actual disorder, but it has sunk deep into men's minds. Look what is going on amongst the working classes, who I admit are tranquil at present. It is true that they are not tormented by political passions as such, to the extent that they once were; but do you not see that their passions, from being political, have become social? Do you not see that little by little opinions and ideas are spreading in their midst which are not aimed simply at overturning this or that law or ministry or government, but at society itself, shaking it to the very foundations on which it rests today? Do you not see that little by little it is being said amongst them that everybody above them is incapable and unworthy of governing, that the division of goods made in the world up to now is unjust, and that property is based on foundations which are inequitable? And do you not think that when such opinions take root, when they spread in a manner which is almost general, when they penetrate deeply into the masses, they bring sooner or later, I do not know how or when, but they bring sooner or later the most dreadful revolutions? Such is my profound conviction, gentlemen. I believe that at this moment we are sleeping on a volcano. . . .

Legislative changes have been suggested. I am very much inclined to think that such changes are not only desirable but necessary; hence I believe in electoral reform. But I am not so foolish, gentlemen, as to fail to see that it is not . . . the mechanism of the laws which produces great events. What produces these events, gentlemen, is the inner spirit of the government. Keep the laws as they are if you wish. I think you would be very wrong to do so, but keep them. Keep the men, too, if it gives you any pleasure; I raise no objection. But in God's name change the spirit of the government; for, I repeat, that spirit is leading you to the abyss.

Arch. parl., Chambre des Députés, 27 January 1848

5 The final banquet

(a) *The* National's *manifesto*

The majority of opposition deputies, disenchanted with the banquet campaign, gave up the idea of holding a final banquet in Paris. In January 1848, however, the idea was adopted by a group of citizens and National Guardsmen of the 12th arrondissement, who proposed not only to hold a bigger and cheaper banquet than ever before but to precede it with a protest march. A number of left-wing deputies, including Lamartine, Garnier-Pagès, Ledru-Rollin, Duvergier de Hauranne, and Odilon Barrot, the leader of the parliamentary opposition, agreed to attend. The government, however, declared the demonstration illegal, and fearing a head-on clash the opposition deputies persuaded the organizing Committee to accept a compromise. The demonstrators would enter the banqueting hall, drink a toast to reform, then retire and try the case in the courts. Unfortunately Armand Marrast (1801-52), the secretary to the Banquet Committee, was still determined to make the most of the occasion. His position as editor of a republican daily newspaper, the *National*, gave him scope for publicity, and on 21 February 1848 he published the following manifesto, spread across three columns on the front page of the newspaper.

REFORM DEMONSTRATION

The general committee charged with organizing the banquet of the 12th arrondissement feels it must remind people that the demonstration fixed for Tuesday next has as its object the lawful and peaceful exercise of a constitutional right, the right of public meeting, without which representative government would be a mere mockery.

Since the government has declared in the tribune that the practice of this right is subject to the discretion of the police, deputies of the opposition, peers of France, former deputies, members of general councils, officers and men of the National Guard, members of the central committee of opposition voters, and editors of national newspapers have accepted the invitation offered to them of taking part in a demonstration in order to protest, in legal fashion, against an illegal and arbitrary pretension.

Since it is reasonable to assume that this public protest will attract a considerable crowd of citizens, and also that the National Guard of Paris, faithful to their device of Liberty and Order, will wish on this occasion to accomplish their twofold duty, defending liberty by joining in the demonstration and protecting law and order and preventing any disturbance by their presence; also that in organising a large gathering of National Guards and citizens it seems desirable to make arrangements which will remove any chance of trouble and disorder; the committee has decided that the demonstration should take place in a quarter of the capital where the roads and squares are spacious enough to allow of people collecting without causing a blockage.

To this end the deputies, peers of France, and other persons invited to the banquet are to assemble on Tuesday next at 11 a.m. at the usual place for meetings of the parliamentary opposition, No. 2, Place de la Madeleine. Subscribers to the banquet who are members of the National Guard are asked to meet in front of the church of the Madeleine and to form two parallel lines between which the guests will take their places. The procession will be headed by such superior officers of the National Guard as present themselves to join in the demonstration. Immediately after the guests and the banqueteers will come a row of officers of the National Guard; behind them the National Guards formed into columns according to the number of their legion; between the third and fourth columns the students from the colleges, under the direction of commissaires chosen by themselves; then the other National Guards of Paris and the suburbs in the order specified above.

The procession will depart at 11.30 a.m., proceeding via the Place de la Concorde and the Champs Élysées to the banqueting hall. The committee, firmly believing that the demonstration will be the more effective if it is calm and the more imposing if it avoids any sign of disorder, urges citizens not to shout slogans or carry flags or banners, and asks the National Guards taking part in the demonstration to come unarmed. The aim is to make a lawful and peaceful protest which will be powerful above all because of the number and the calm and tranquil attitude of the participants.

The committee hopes that under these circumstances every man present will regard himself as an official charged with the maintenance of law and order. It is relying on the presence of the National Guards; it is relying on the sentiments of the people of Paris, who want peace along with liberty and who know that to ensure the maintenance of their rights they need only to make a peaceful demonstration such as befits an intelligent and enlightened nation, aware of the irresistible authority of its moral force and sure of making its rightful wishes prevail by the legal and calm expression of its opinion.

National, 21 February 1848

(c) *The government's stand*

Marrast's manifesto seriously alarmed the government, which decided to stop play-acting and ban the demonstration in earnest. This decision was made clear by Duchâtel, Minister of the Interior, in the course of an emergency debate in the Chamber. The majority of opposition deputies withdrew their support from the banquet, and the National Guards were distinctly hesitant, but a group of revolutionary activists encouraged the students to go on with the procession. The resentment caused by the government's efforts to put a stop to the affair brought about the downfall not only of the Guizot ministry but of the July Monarchy.

Duchâtel: I shall tell the Chamber briefly and clearly what the attitude of the government is and what ground it takes its stand on. The honourable M. Odilon Barrot has said that the question of unlimited right of meeting has been discussed in this Chamber and no decision arrived at; that he wants a solution and that it was to obtain this solution that the project of a banquet was announced and prepared. He added that the government itself appeared disposed, as far as it was concerned and as far as it could see, to bring about the judicial solution which would have ended the debate. That is true. . . . But, gentlemen, the circumstances have changed. There cannot be a single person in this Chamber who has not read, this morning, a manifesto published by a committee whose members are not named, inserted in all the opposition newspapers. What does this manifesto say? It does not confine itself to instigating a banquet and preparing the judicial solution in question. No; it puts out an appeal to all those who share the principles of the opposition, inviting them to a demonstration which I do not hesitate to say would compromise the tranquillity of the city. And that is not all. The manifesto provokes the National Guard, in defiance of the law, in defiance of the Act of 1831, to assemble as National Guards; and not only does it provoke the National Guard but it invites the young men from the colleges, minors, who should be occupying themselves with their studies, to join in the procession, which will be lined by National Guards of the 12th legion. It announces that the National Guards will be placed according to the order of their legions and commanded by their superior officers. This manifesto violates all the laws of the country on which tranquillity and public order depend. . . . The Riot Act is violated[3]; the law on the National Guard is violated. I put it to the impartial feeling of this Chamber: what is this manifesto if it is not the proclamation of a government wishing to place itself alongside the regular government; a government born of a committee that I do not know and cannot attempt to describe, taking the place of the constitutional government founded on the Charter and supported by the majority of the two Chambers? The government set up by this committee speaks to the citizens, convokes the National Guard on its own initiative, provokes an illegal assembly in defiance of the law. Such a thing is insupportable; we ought not to allow it. It is our responsibility to maintain law and order.

Arch. parl., *Chambre des Députés*, 21 February
1848

[3] *Loi sur les attroupements.*

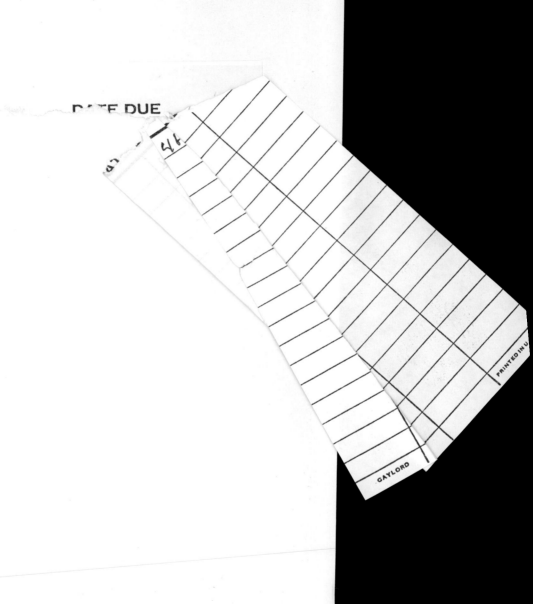